The Ethnic Crucible

The Ethnic Crucible:
Harmony and Hostility in Multi-Ethnic Schools

by

Gajendra Verma, Paul Zec and George Skinner

 The Falmer Press

(A member of the Taylor & Francis Group)
London • Washington, D.C.

UK   The Falmer Press, 4 John Street, London WC1N 2ET
USA   The Falmer Press, Taylor & Francis Inc., 1900 Frost Road, Suite 101,
        Bristol, PA 19007

First published in 1994

A catalogue record for this book is available from the British Library

Library of Congress Cataloging-in-Publication Data are available on request

ISBN 0 7507 0377 6 cased
ISBN 0 7507 0378 4 paper

Jacket design by Caroline Archer

Typeset in 10/12pt Times by
Graphicraft Typesetters Ltd., Hong Kong.

Printed in Great Britain by Burgess Science Press, Basingstoke on paper which has a specified pH value on final paper manufacture of not less than 7.5 and is therefore 'acid free'.

Contents

List of Tables

Preface

Many schools in developed countries have children and adolescents from a variety of ethnic, linguistic, religious and cultural backgrounds. They relate to each other in various degrees of encounter that range from harmony to hostility. Harmonious inter-ethnic relations cannot be taken for granted and how they can be fostered remains problematic. On the other hand, inter-ethnic hostility can take many forms: prejudice, racism, sexism, covert and overt discrimination, harassment and even physical violence. Examples of these are presented in this book. The features of bad inter-ethnic relationships may, of course, be manifestations of inequalities in the wider society that are brought into the school.

The research on which this book is based was carried out in nine secondary schools — five in the Greater Manchester area and four in the London area. It sought to provide a portrait of relationships in the schools studied in terms of their organisation, structures and interactive processes. It attempted to characterise prevalent attitudes and behaviour, centring on those of the students and those who taught them. The study further sought to discover how inter-ethnic relationships are influenced by the policies and practices of individual schools. The earlier piloting of the research instruments in two schools gave us some confidence that research of this kind could yield positive models and examples of good school practice which might be of help to schools with a multi-ethnic population.

The rationale of the research was rooted in five basic assumptions:

i)   that the condition of inter-ethnic relations in the UK continues to be a matter of concern;

ii)   that inter-ethnic tension and conflict are correlated with racial prejudice and discrimination;

iii) that the educational system constitutes an important focus for consideration of the connected phenomena of inter-ethnic conflict and racial discrimination;

iv)   that there is a clear connection between inter-ethnic relationships on the one hand, and educational opportunities and attainments of students of ethnic minority origin on the other;

v)   that 'good inter-ethnic relationships', interpreted positively, means more than the mere absence of overt hostility or conflict between persons or groups (a negative interpretation). The phrase suggests, *inter alia*: substantial and reciprocal knowledge and understanding of ways of life between student groups of different ethnicity and between teachers and students; substantially shared values concerning, for example, respect for persons, tolerance, rights and duties, together with public commitment to such values throughout a school; and a considerable degree of positive interaction between persons and groups of different ethnicity.

This last element in the research's rationale reflects our intention that the study should enable us to discern factors in the schools which tend to promote good inter-ethnic relationships. Specifically, as a result of this study, and through the dissemination of its findings, it is hoped that those involved in the shaping or execution of policy in schools will have access to:

- a better understanding of the issues, problems and opportunities associated with inter-ethnic relationships;
- a clearer grasp of which of those issues etc. are capable of being addressed by the school;
- a sharper awareness of the factors which promote good inter-ethnic relationships; and
- a basis for a more systematic and pro-active approach to the practicalities of inter-ethnic relationships, in such contexts as formal and 'hidden' curricula, staff development, pastoral regimes, cultural life in the school, school-community relationships and communication with parents.

We hope that the findings presented in the book will be accessible to teachers, teacher trainers, educational decision-makers, parents and others interested in and responsible for the education of *all*.

The research process was essentially *ethnographic* in emphasis. That is to say, it sought to yield its insights largely through recording the perceptions, opinions and conceptual categories of those who work in the schools and who experience one facet or another of inter-ethnic relations. The meaning and significance of in-school processes and events, and the classification of groups, are, as far as possible, received by the researchers *from* what people say, rather than imposed by the researchers *upon* what people say. The study was, therefore, a series of detailed case studies, and its potential value was dependent on the use of research instruments which were compatible with the ethnographic approach. However, the fact that as many as nine schools have been studied in this way, together with the administration of a questionnaire to a large number of students across the nine schools, does inject a quantitative dimension to the data which is helpful as a back-cloth against which to place the ethnographic data. Furthermore, the researchers' own observations (in formal and informal situations) have been seen as a necessary additional dimension.

This book is an edited, and in parts virtually rewritten, version of the report submitted to the sponsors of the research, the Leverhulme Trust. All conclusions expressed in the book reflect our own interpretation of the data.

In the last chapter of the book we suggest some ways in which schools can work towards good inter-ethnic relationships. This is an aim not confined to British conditions, but with wider applicability. We thus intend this book to transcend parochial concerns, and hope that it will contribute towards a better understanding of inter-ethnic relationships in pluralist societies.

Gajendra Verma
Paul Zec
George Skinner
1994

Acknowledgments

In a study such as this one is conscious of the fact that many people have provided support, information and assistance at different stages of the research.

First among those must be the Leverhulme Trust who, by its generous grant, made the research possible. No research is possible without funding, from one source or another, and that, in itself, is an occasion for sincere thanks to the Trust.

Second we must thank the nine schools in the Greater Manchester and London areas who formed the nucleus of the research, and shared their experiences and views on a very sensitive but important aspect of education. The demands of confidentiality have meant that the schools, students, headteachers, teachers and others who participated in this research cannot be named or adequately thanked publicly. However, it would have been impossible to accomplish this work without their cooperation and generous help. These schools allowed us unlimited access to all aspects of their institutional life throughout our research. Students who participated in this research deserve our heartfelt appreciation and thanks for their tolerance, cooperation and insight. Much that was thought-provoking in the material yielded by the research originated in students' remarks to us. We are also grateful to the staff and students of Sharples School, Bolton and White Hart Lane Comprehensive School, London, who provided invaluable help with the designing and piloting of research instruments.

We should like to thank Ms Deborah Gewirtz who worked as Research Associate on the research project. We would also like to express our thanks to members of the Advisory Group for their valuable theoretical and practical insight. We, however, bear full responsibility for the final product.

We are grateful to the Governors and Principal of Canterbury Christ Church College for their financial and logistical support, and to the University of Manchester for providing administrative and computer facilities.

Finally, we should like to express our gratitude to Ms Janet Grimshaw who gave untiring administrative support to the research project and who, with Ms Donna Cunningham, gave many hours to the production of the manuscript for this book.

Chapter 1

An Historical Prologue

The primary concern of this study is to consider the nature and quality of inter-ethnic relationships among students in multi-ethnic schools and the impact school policies and practices may have on them. However, it would seem impossible to understand such relationships without some reference to the broader historical context and issues of interaction between communities in British society at large.

There has hardly been a time when British society was not to some degree multi-cultural or multi-ethnic. Parekh (1990) has rightly argued that the nature of this historic diversity differs in both degree and nature from Britain's present plural society. None the less, it provides an important backcloth to twentieth-century developments and undermines the myth that issues of race and culture have only arisen because of post-war immigration. Britain has long consisted of the ethnic communities of England, Scotland and Wales. Its close proximity to Ireland has ensured that there has been an Irish presence for centuries, so much so that today the largest 'immigrant' community in England remains the Irish. In terms of a wider European presence, as the Swann Report observed, 'Italians have been coming to this country ever since the Roman invasion!' (DES, 1985).

There was also a significant black and Asian presence in Britain long before post-war large-scale immigration. There were sufficient 'negroes and blackamoors' living in Elizabethan England for Queen Elizabeth I to express concern at the threat she felt they posed to the wider welfare of the nation. There is good evidence from contemporary documents to suggest that there were as many as 20,000 Negro servants living in London in the 1760s. Indian links with Europe go back some 10,000 years and, more formally with Britain, from the end of the sixteenth century. Since the end of the seventeenth century, ayahs (servants), lascars (sailors) and princes have been present in Britain in small numbers. By the middle of the nineteenth century there were already the beginnings of an Asian community in Britain. Although comprising mainly migrant workers there were also entrepreneurs, including eye doctors and other professionals. As Visram (1986) observes, 'One of the major legacies of the British control of India was the planting of peoples of Indian origin all over the British Empire, including Britain itself'.

In terms of religious diversity, Britain has had a Jewish presence since the times of the Norman conquest and despite recurring anti-semitism, some Jews remained throughout the middle ages. A small community of Sephardic Jews was established in Britain in the seventeenth century after their expulsion from Spain. Towards the end of the last century this established and prosperous community grew substantially with the immigration of mainly poorer 'Ashkenazi' Jews fleeing the Czarist Empire. By the middle of the nineteenth century the Jewish community was running its own schools.

Though much is often made today of the high profile of some black or Asian individuals in current social, cultural or political spheres, there have been for centuries some (albeit very few) examples of outstanding and, in their day, well-known ethnic minority public figures. In 1892, Dadabhai Naoroji, a Bombay-born Parsee, was elected to the British House of Commons as Labour MP for Finsbury Central, sparking off a country-wide debate (not unlike the more recent conflict in Gloucestershire) about the suitability of black candidates. Three years later, Mancherjee Bhownaggee, another Parsee, won Bethnal Green North East for the Conservatives. In sport K.S. Ranjitsinhji was champion batsman for the English cricket team in 1896 and toured Australia in the 1897–8 season as a member of the English party. Jamaican-born Mary Secole became a household name in Victorian Britain for medical services for Britain in the Crimean war and her book recounting her 'adventures' became a best seller. Yet today she is largely unknown and as the publishers of a recent reprint of her autobiography put it 'Mary Secole deserves to stand beside Florence Nightingale, but is seldom accorded even a footnote' (Alexander and Dewjee, 1984). There are others who are remembered but whose ethnic origins are not always recognised. The novelist and politician Benjamin Disraeli who served as Prime Minister on two occasions in the second half of the nineteenth century came from a Jewish family. Composer Samuel Coleridge-Taylor was born to mixed African and English parents and spent much of his life experiencing, and campaigning against, racial prejudice.

It is worth noting at this point how few outstanding black, Asian and other ethnic minority figures have remained heroes of traditional British culture. As Tomlinson (1989) argues, this must be due in part to the imperialistic and ethnocentric biases behind both the schools' curriculum, which has dominated British education for 150 years, and popular children's literature since the late nineteenth century. It is impossible to estimate the long term impact of such influences on national self-perception but it is unlikely that educational responses alone are likely to do much to change the attitudes and perceptions of the parents and grandparents of pupils in school today.

Large-scale Immigration

As has been shown, the impression sometimes given that Britain has suddenly become a plural society is clearly not accurate. However, it is true that Asian and black people have been present only in relatively small numbers until the twentieth century.

The 1920s and 1930s saw the arrival of Sikhs, many of whom took up door to door selling. No ethnic statistics existed in Britain before the 1960s but the 1932 Indian National Congress survey of Indians outside India estimated that there were 7,128 Indians in the United Kingdom (Visram, 1986). Although Chinese have been present in Britain in small numbers since the nineteenth century they were largely single males (often ex-seamen) and at the turn of the century estimates suggest numbers in the order of five hundred. The Swann Report (DES, 1985) suggests that 80 per cent of the present Chinese estimated population of 100,000 in Britain (mainly drawn originally from rural agricultural areas of Hong Kong's New Territories) have arrived in the last twenty years. Similarly, the vast majority of Britain's 140,000-strong Cypriot community came in the 1950s and 1960s mainly for economic and political reasons in the years leading up to independence and British withdrawal.

Most significant of all in terms of numbers has been the post Second World War increase in immigration of South Asian and New Commonwealth families. In the 1950s and 1960s, a combination of 'push' and 'pull' factors drew people to Britain from many Commonwealth countries. The poverty of some West Indian communities, combined with the need for workers in industry and public transport, resulted in an effective campaign by London Transport and other bodies to bring Afro-Caribbeans from the West Indies. The demise of the cotton industry in India and the opportunities of the textile mills in the North and Midlands drew people from North-West India and Pakistan. Internal conflicts on the Indian subcontinent and in East Africa caused others to seek a new home in their Commonwealth's 'mother country'. Unlike the European 'guestworker', most of these immigrants came to Britain on British passports and with full legal rights to settle here.

Some immigrants followed the traditional pattern of father followed by mother followed by children. Others, especially those escaping persecution, came as families. Some came in groups from single villages with little or no formal education. Others, particularly Gujeratis, were continuing the long established tradition of emigration based on a historic entrepreneurial spirit. For some immigrants, settling in Britain was seen as a short term measure to earn money to support families at home before returning at an appropriate time. This 'myth of return' persists, not only among Asian communities such as Muslims in Rochdale (Anwar, 1979) but also among Cypriot families (DES, 1985).

The reaction to this large-scale immigration was initially mixed. Welcomed by industry, patronised by the media (as contemporary Pathé newsreels demonstrate), feared by the unions and regarded with much suspicion and even superstition by society at large, immigrants established themselves in communities throughout Britain. The British sense of superiority established during colonial rule largely continued, as is illustrated by an opinion poll conducted in 1967 which revealed that three-fifths of white British people considered themselves superior to Africans and Asians.

However, by the early 1960s, the changed economic situation and inner-city racial tension had already begun to fuel a more sinister response to immigration. The reaction of the Conservative government was the Commonwealth Immigrants Act of 1962 which qualified the right of free entry to the UK for migrants from the New Commonwealth and marked the end of what had been largely a *laissez-faire* approach to immigration. Though initially opposed to such developments, the succeeding Labour government extended the Act, using the argument that, in the words of Roy Hattersley, 'without integration, limitation is inexcusable; without limitation, integration is impossible'.

By the late 1960s the 'numbers' issue was being hotly debated. In 1967 several fascist groups united to form the National Front as a means of more effectively influencing immigration policy through political elections. Although National Front candidates have failed to win substantial support in elections, two members of the breakaway National Party were elected to Blackburn Council ten years later. In 1968 Enoch Powell made his infamous 'rivers of blood' speech to Conservative party members in Birmingham. 'We must be mad,' he argued, 'literally mad, as a nation to be permitting the annual inflow of some 50,000 dependants, who are for the most part the material of the future growth of the immigrant-descended population'. The timing of the speech ensured a wide hearing and though it cost Powell his place in the Conservative party shadow cabinet it won widespread support, including a 'We Back Powell' strike supported by, among others, dockers. It has been argued that the Powell 'earthquake' set the terms for all future debates on immigration and 'his version of the reality of race relations has now been firmly appropriated as the basis for intervention on this issue by many leading politicians' (Troyna, 1984b). Certainly the eagerness to appease the anxieties of the white population can be seen in more recent political concern to promote 'the British way of life' and in the sympathy expressed by Margaret Thatcher for those white British people who felt that their way of life was being 'swamped' by other cultures.

Recent legislation in Britain has made immigration even more difficult. While small numbers of South Asians (mainly from Bangladesh) continue to arrive in Britain and (literally) immigrant children arrive in schools, an ever increasing proportion of black and Asian pupils are British born.

Britain was by no means alone in having to meet such a challenge. In Europe, by the nineteenth century, recognition of linguistic, cultural and religious diversity was already marked. In countries such as France and Germany in particular, great efforts were made to acculturate divergent cultural groups into the dominant culture and language. In spite of those efforts, the European nation states always retained within their political boundaries very substantial ethnic minorities, whose cultures varied significantly from that of the dominant state. The settlements made at the end of the First World War attempted to establish culturally homogeneous nation states, insofar as their creation was consistent with the interests of the major powers. However, cultural diversity within individual states was not eliminated and, in some cases, their creation only served to accentuate it. Considerable differences in value orientation, beliefs, and lifestyle are still apparent between the European countries.

The Ethnic Minority Presence

Many misconceptions exist concerning the size, growth and composition of ethnic minority groups living in the UK. It is often overlooked that half of the ethnic minority population was born in Britain and nearly three-quarters are British citizens. While many schools have responded to the changing social patterns, there is still

much ignorance and misunderstanding among young people. A study of inter-
ethnic relations in schools carried out by Verma (1992) showed that schools containing considerable numbers of pupils from ethnic minority groups were much
more advanced in developing school policies on race relations than schools with
few such pupils. This study also found that 'few teachers were at all knowledgeable
about the religions, cultures, values and customs of the ethnic minority groups of
their pupils. Often this was attributed to the fact that, with very few exceptions,
issues of ethnicity and culture formed no part of their initial training'. Yet it is not
unreasonable to assume that ignorance provides a ready breeding ground for prejudice
and racism.

Table 1.1: Estimated size of total ethnic minority population in Great Britain, 1951–1991

	1951	1961	1971	1981	1991
N (thousands)	200	500	1,200	2,100	3,006
% age of total population	0.4	1.0	2.3	3.9	5.5

Sources: Shaw, 1988, Table 2; Haskey, 1990, Table 1; OPCS, 1992; Owen, 1992

Table 1.2: Population of Great Britain by ethnic group based on the 1991 census (in thousands)

	N (000's)	% age	Rank size order based on N
White	51,843	94.5	1
All ethnic minorities	3,006	5.5	
South Asian	1,477	2.7	
Indian	841	1.5	2
Pakistani	476	0.9	4
Bangladeshi	160	0.3	9
Black	885	1.6	
Caribbean	499	0.9	3
African	207	0.4	6
Other	179	0.3	8
Chinese and others	644	1.2	
Chinese	157	0.3	9
Other Asian	197	0.4	7
Other minority groups	290	0.5	5

Until the 1990 census, accurate statistics about Britain's plural society were
not easily come by. Previous to 1990, census statistics only indicated the place of
birth of the head of household thereby failing to identify those ethnic minority
households where the head had been born in Britain. The latest census allows for
identification of cultural diversity and Tables 1.1 and 1.2 draw on this data to
provide a clearer picture of the size and distribution of ethnic minority communities
in the UK. Britain's minority communities are diverse and complex. There are
religious communities (for example Muslims) which cut across cultural and racial
groupings. The Muslim community quite rightly took Swann to task for its persistent use of 'ethnic minority' when speaking of the British Muslim communities
(Islamic Academy, 1985).

There are communities which share a common linguistic or geographical heritage which may unite beyond religious or other differences. One such example is Britain's Gujerati community which consists of orthodox Muslims and associated sects (Ismailis, Bhoras and Ishnasheris), a range of Hindu groups and a small number of Jains and Parsees. Despite this, contributors to the Anniversary Issue of the Gujarat Samachar were able to speak of the 'collective Gujarati consciousness' (Vyas, 1983).

Some communities, including the Chinese and certain European groups, are dispersed throughout almost every town and village of Britain and until recently have had a relatively limited corporate voice. Others are more closely identified with specific towns or districts (like the Jews in London, Leeds and Manchester). Many black communities are found almost entirely in the inner-city areas forming what has been described as an 'underclass' of modern society (Rex and Tomlinson, 1979). There are minority communities of European origin, the 'invisible immigrants' such as Poles, Italians and Cypriots, often overlooked in discussions about pluralism and education (King, 1979). Furthermore, the evidence about inter-racial marriages suggests that an increasing proportion of young people will see themselves belonging possibly to two or three communities — or none at all (Bagley, 1972).

The pattern is further complicated by the varying degrees of separatism or integration within communities, the tension between orthodoxy and radicalism within religious groups, and the search for and rediscovery of linguistic, religious or racial roots of second and third generation immigrants who might otherwise have been largely assimilated into mainstream British culture. The pattern is dynamic. It is influenced by the attitudes and power of the dominant cultural groups as well as by the developing (or ossifying) cultures within minority groups. It is clearly important to avoid simplistic descriptions or interpretations of ethnicity. Diversity exists not only between communities but within them. Generalisations about beliefs, practices and experiences have only limited value (Verma, 1986). The experience of acceptance or rejection by members of these many groups also varies. The Swann Report (DES, 1985) argued that 'the Chinese community does not appear to have been subjected to racism to the same extent as some other ethnic minority communities'. The factors which the Report suggested may have been responsible for this include, 'their intentionally low profile, their lack of concentration in any particular area, and also the fact that they are seen to be performing a useful function through providing Chinese restaurants and are not competing in the mainstream jobs market'. More recent research indicates that such explanations are simplistic and that the Chinese community has experienced quite direct racism in some situations. However, patterns of racism do seem to vary in relation to the function of different ethnic groups. Whereas colour may be the key factor in racism against Asian and black minorities, it is not the only factor as is demonstrated by the fact that those of European origin often encounter forms of racism. The Swann Report spoke of 'considerable evidence' of experience of racism from members of the Cypriot community and among pupils of Italian origin. Indeed, the Report's section on 'other ethnic minorities' observes that among the common factors shared by all groups 'is, regrettably, the influence of racism on their lives'. Not all racial or ethnic tension is *between* dominant and minority cultures. There is evidence of prejudice between some minority communities, as in the case of some Cypriot and Italian attitudes towards minority groups in general, and between groups within minority communities.

Prejudice, Racism and Racialism ✕

The pattern of relationships between dominant and minority communities in society can be complex. Swann (*op. cit.*) speaks of two pole positions which such relationships might take — assimilation, in which minority groups lose all distinctive characteristics, and separatism, in which minority communities exist in the same society but with the absolute minimum of contact in order to coexist. As Berry (1979) demonstrates, relationships depend on the responses of both dominant and minority communities. Such relationships, and the need for their formal acceptance into national policy, is an international phenomenon and countries have adopted different responses to multi-culturalism (Lynch, 1989). Berry (1979) defines four contrasted situations. *Integration* exists when a distinct identity and culture is linked to the general wish of society to maintain positive inter-ethnic relations. When the dominant group does not wish to maintain positive relations with minority groups, *separatism* emerges. When the feelings of the dominant group are positive, and the particular ethnic group has no wish to retain a separate cultural identity, *assimilation* takes place. When no separate identity is sought, but when the majority group is hostile to the minority group, the result is *marginality*. In Britain, the intellectual debate about appropriate models of pluralism (see below) continues. In the meantime, the abiding experience of ethnic minorities is one of prejudice and racial discrimination with, according to a recent report of the European Parliament, a racist attack made on average every 26 minutes (*The Guardian*, 24 July 1990).

At this point it is appropriate to clarify what we understand by such terms as 'prejudice' and 'racism'. Prejudice refers to either favourable or unfavourable attitudes, feelings and beliefs that have been constructed without prior knowledge, understanding and reason. The prime characteristic of prejudice is its irrationality; a mind closed to evidence supporting conflicting views. All of us acquire a range of prejudices through the socialisation process of the family, peer group, school, neighbourhood and wider society. When individuals and groups are competing for power and resources, the potential for prejudice to function is high. That propensity is further heightened when resources (e.g. in employment, housing, health care and educational opportunity) are not sufficient to meet the expectations developed by society. Positive prejudices are largely focused on circumstances where groups hold views and a set of values that command the individual's allegiance. Unfavourable prejudices are directed at those who do not conform to such views and values.

Racism involves the combination of prejudice with the ability or power to subordinate other individuals or groups, either consciously or otherwise. Needless to say, in most situations in the UK, minority groups are relatively powerless.

Racism, both personal and institutional, is not just a recent feature of British society. As early as 1601 Queen Elizabeth I issued a Royal Proclamation to deport black people. The main ground for deportation was economic, during what was described in the proclamation as 'hard times of dearth', but there was also a clear religious dimension, the Queen expressing concern that most of these black people were 'infidels having no understanding of Christ or His Gospel'. Four centuries earlier, Britain's Jewish community had experienced terrible persecution leading finally to official expulsion in 1290.

Britain's colonial past, including almost two and a half centuries of official involvement in the slave trade, provided almost unlimited opportunities for the expression of racist attitudes and behaviour both abroad and at home. In many ways the experience of black and Asian people in Britain today is still determined by the legacy of the Empire and the national perception of other races and cultures at all levels:

> The experiences of Asians in Britain in the period before 1947 were similar to those of later arrivals and of the black community in general. As subject peoples from colonial India, they faced patronizing 'concern' and apathy, and had to endure the racist stereotyped perceptions of the British . . . In this respect, the experiences of Asians in Britain today have a long history (Visram, 1986).

And as Tomlinson (1990) comments:

> The background to American race relations is that of slavery — the background to British urban race relations is that of colonialism, with the unpleasant racial beliefs and stereotypes developed during the period of Empire, underpinning new racial antagonism.

Today, race relations in Britain form part of the complex pattern of urban living, impinging on a wide range of social issues and provision including housing, employment, policing, social services, youth work as well as education. In these and other areas of life, ethnic minority groups continue to experience the impact of racism, not least in the lack of access to resources. While national and local government legislation has gone some way to working towards equality of opportunity, stimulated in part by the fear of urban unrest in the late 1970s and 1980s, there is still no whole-hearted commitment to total reform. Tomlinson concludes her review of policies and practices influencing minority communities in urban Britain by suggesting that it will be a long time before policies and practices produce a positive impact on the lives of ethnic minorities. 'The political will to create such conditions is lacking — for the long-standing reason that politicians of all parties fear a racist reaction from the white British public. . . .' Yet as Pumfrey and Verma (1990) argue, 'there are policies and practices that reduce rather than exacerbate inter-ethnic tensions. We can make choices'.

The mass media continues to perpetuate popular myths about racial minorities.

Television and newspapers have made some progress in opening up opportunities for ethnic minority expression and have been involved in some self-evaluation with regard to the presentation of race issues. Yet despite the creation in 1976 by the National Union of Journalists of the Campaign Against Racism in the Media there is little evidence to suggest that the media have gone far in combating racist or stereotypical images (Verma and Darby, 1990):

> On the contrary, despite the Race Relations Act of 1976, the press is essentially unchanged in its treatment of issues of race. It continues to write its stories in such a way as to reinforce racial prejudice and notions that black people are inferior to white (*ibid.*, p. 197).

Careless reporting may continue to perpetuate misconceptions. A recent report on the 24-hour Asian radio station Sunrise Radio in the Independent newspaper, though carefully and objectively written, included a statement that the station 'will now be able to reach an estimated *eight million* Asians in the UK' (Wroe, 1991).

Beyond the institutional failure to respond fully to racism is the experience of direct racism. It is difficult to gather accurate data about daily incidents of racism. However, the CRE (1987) report on racial attacks argued that the evidence they were able to obtain indicates that there had been a steady overall increase in the levels of racial harassment. It is also possible to record the concerted efforts of groups like the National Front, the British Movement and the British National Party to promote racial unrest. Although the National Front has sought to do this largely (though without success) through the ballot box, the British Movement has concentrated on attracting white working-class males, making full use of youth cultures such as the 'skinheads' to promote racism, particularly through large gatherings such as soccer games and rock concerts.

Political Responses

Kirp's (1979) survey of British political responses to race and racism, 'Doing Good by Doing Little', demonstrated how, unlike the USA, successive British governments have adopted a low key approach to issues of race. This policy of 'racial inexplicitness' by which governments 'sought to do good by stealth' continued into the 1980s. In the words of Shirley Williams (1989):

> Perceiving themselves to be tolerant, many Britons felt that there was no need to embark upon legislation and administrative action to combat racism . . . It would all work out all right.

From the 1960s on, two key issues concerned central government: the control of immigration and the prevention of racial discrimination. In 1962 the Commonwealth Immigrants Act was passed, solely concerned with the control of entry and settlement of immigrants. In 1965, the white paper 'Immigration from the

Commonwealth' (HMSO, 1965), whilst recommending even closer control of immigration, made the first steps towards promoting good community relations between the host and immigrant communities. In the same year, the Race Relations Board was created, though given little power, and racial incitement was made a criminal offence.

Both aspects of central government concern were tackled in 1966 with the passing of the Commonwealth Immigrants Act (which removed the right of entry of British East African Asians) and the Race Relations Act. Despite clear legislation about direct and indirect racial discrimination, the Act lacked any real power. The Community Relations Commission (later absorbed into the Commission for Racial Equality) created by the Act also had no power to act, only to persuade. Further control of immigration was established by the 1969 Immigration Appeals Act and the 1971 Immigration Act, the latter empowering the Home Secretary to make further immigration rules as he saw fit. The British Nationality Act of 1981, despite its title, was effectively a further immigration law.

By the early 1970s it had become increasingly apparent that further measures were needed to combat direct and indirect discrimination in society. In 1976 a new Race Relations Act was passed, providing a wider definition of unlawful discrimination and giving greater powers to the Commission for Racial Equality. The CRE was given the responsibility for ensuring the implementation and monitoring of the Act. In practice, combining the role of a law-enforcing agency and educational body has proved an almost impossible task for the Commission. Proposals made in the two reviews of the Act (CRE, 1985, 1992) have received little or no formal response from the government. As the 1992 review comments 'racial discrimination remains widespread and pernicious . . . and so far from being redundant the Race Relations Act as at present formulated does not provide a strong enough basis for dealing with it'.

Issues of education of immigrant children had not gone unnoticed in this process but the 1972/3 recommendations by the Select Committee on Race Relations and Immigration (SCORRI) were largely ignored by the government which wished to tackle issues of ethnicity and education under an overall response to educational disadvantage. The general requirements of the 1976 Race Relations Act applied to education and Section 18(1) makes explicit the responsibility of LEAs to avoid racial discrimination in carrying out their functions. By 1976 SCORRI had identified as a matter of urgency the continuing underachievement of West Indian pupils in schools and in 1977 called for the setting up of an independent enquiry. The Labour government set up the Committee of Inquiry (the 'Rampton', and later, 'Swann' Committee) in 1979.

The findings of the Inquiry will be taken up again in other sections of this book. At this point it is worth noting that the political commitment shown in initiating the inquiry was never to be matched in supporting or implementing its findings. The contributors to Verma's (1989) collection of papers *Education for All: A Landmark in Pluralism* reflect a variety of views about the Swann Report but many share one common theme of grave doubts about its political implementation. In the words of Rex, 'Government statements in response to Swann have been

evasive and have not given any resources towards the implementation of its programme'. Indeed, commenting on the absence of a full government response to its
Interim Report, the Committee of Inquiry itself stated:

> The absence of a full response to our interim report, which was specific-
> ally requested by the government, can also perhaps be regarded as evid-
> ence of the extent of genuine concern and commitment to this field of
> work . . . (DES, 1985, p. 220).

Verma concludes:

> Time is slipping away. Government policies have yet to be clearly defined
> and the machinery has yet to be put in place which will result in a reduc-
> tion in racial prejudice and discrimination not only in educational institu-
> tions but in society at large (*op. cit.*).

The 1980s also saw the development of more local government equal opportunities
policies (Troyna, 1990; Tomlinson, 1989). In effect, the continuing national urban
regeneration policies and projects also benefit ethnic minorities in particular (four-
fifths of whom live in such areas) but government policy continues to adopt a
largely colour-blind approach to issues of urban renewal.

In practice, the educational experience of most ethnic minority pupils and
parents is part of their wider experience of urban and national life. The political
response to both minority needs and to racism in its various forms is clearly a key
factor in influencing that experience for good or ill. The Swann Report (DES, 1985)
argued that the impact of racism in schools could not be understood without reference to 'the general climate of racism in this country' and includes in this both
institutional forms (e.g. housing, employment and health care) as well as direct and
personal forms such as racial harassment and attacks. This is well illustrated by a
recent report (TES, 25 February, 1994) showing that on London's Isle of Dogs
racial incidents have increased 300 per cent since September 1993 when Derek
Beackon, a member of the British National Party, was elected as a councillor for
this borough. Pupils (primarily Asian) of one particular school were being trans-
ferred to other schools because of the impact of racial harassment in the area. Fear
of attacks resulted in children not staying on after school for extra-curricular activities and fewer minority parents attending parents' evenings.

The Educational Response to Pluralism

Surveys of educational responses to race and culture in Britain often begin by
tracing a sequence of assimilation, integration and pluralism in mainstream education, starting with post-war immigration (Mullard, 1982; DES, 1985; O'Keefe,
1986). However, the ethnic minority presence in education goes back further and
goes beyond the issues raised about appropriate education in mainstream schools.

Firstly, traditions of supplementary forms of education were well-established in Britain by Jewish communities and the pattern has been followed by European, Asian and Afro-Caribbean groups. Initially aimed at strengthening cultural or religious identity in the face of the threat of cultural assimilation, such community responses today may take many more forms including West Indian Saturday schools, seen primarily as supplementing the inadequacies of mainstream education (Stone, 1981), and the self-defence clubs of the Jewish community set up in response to perceived personal racism.

Secondly, less formal types of education, often associated with places of worship and primarily concerned with religious induction, were also established by Jews and in more recent years the pattern has been followed by particular religious minorities including Muslims, Hindus, Sikhs and Parsees.

Thirdly, there has been a large number of private day schools established in recent years, by Muslim groups in particular (Anwar, 1988). Such schools follow a long tradition of private provision by religious communities. For example, there has been a Jewish school in Manchester since 1834, catering in the late nineteenth century especially for the large numbers of immigrant Jewish children flocking to Britain from Russia and Poland.

Fourthly, the 'dual system' of church and state partnership in education has established the potential for non-Christian religious minorities to establish schools within the maintained system of state education. Alongside Catholic, Methodist and Anglican schools, a significant number of Jewish schools have taken advantage of this historic tradition, enshrined in the 1944 Education Act. The continuing legal provision has been much discussed, not least in the light of the aspiration of some Muslims to follow in the pattern of Christians and Jews (DES, 1985; Halstead, 1986; Skinner, 1990). To date, no other religious group has been able to establish voluntary schools. Whatever the advantages or disadvantages of such a system may be (and opinion is divided within most religious communities as well as among educationalists), it remains a significant dimension of the minority presence within the education scene and contributes to the frustrations and injustices felt by some religious minorities and the intense debate among educationalists and politicians about appropriate educational provision for plural Britain (see, for example, Ball and Troyna, 1987).

The implications of such a variety of educational responses by minority communities go beyond the immediate practical issues. Chazan (1980) has shown, in relation to the Jewish community, that they provide a useful indicator of wider patterns of separatism and assimilation. Such alternative or supplementary provision is an under-resourced and little researched dimension of the education process. What little research has been done indicates a complex pattern of reasons for establishing such forms of education. Included among many positive statements about preserving cultural and religious identity can be found feelings of dissatisfaction with the inadequacy of the mainstream system or concerns about racism, experienced or feared, in schools (Skinner, 1980; Stone, 1981; Clark, 1992). As Stone comments:

What we are seeing in the Saturday schools is the development of a strategy based on action, rather than the acceptance of a passive role by parents and the community in the schooling of their children (*op. cit.*).

Such 'action' is part of a long tradition of ethnic minority commitment to supplementary or alternative educational provision. The suspicion or indifference with which such efforts have often been met have done little to promote confidence among many ethnic minority parents or community leaders/representatives in local or national government.

It is interesting to note that the Department of Education in Dublin has encouraged Islamic education for Muslim children in Ireland (TES, 7 May, 1993). By establishing the Muslim National School in cooperation with the Irish Muslim community, the government has shown its commitment to the 'pluralism of the Irish society'.

Mainstream School Responses

As we have mentioned earlier, one approach to understanding the educational response to Britain's increasingly pluralistic society is to trace the historical development within mainstream provision over the last thirty years.

The initial educational response to immigration in the late 1950s and early 1960s moved from the *laissez faire* attitude already outlined above to attempts at assimilating children from minority communities. Many LEAs developed policies of 'English for immigrants' in response to what was seen as the major educational 'problem'. Some LEAs even attempted to speed up the assimilationist process through 'dispersal policies'. What in effect amounted to systems of 'bussing' ethnic minority pupils between schools were endorsed by the DES who recommended that where necessary 'every effort should be made to disperse the immigrant children round a greater number of schools and to meet such problems of transport as may arise' (DES, 1965). The same circular spoke about 'the successful assimilation of immigrant children'. The philosophy was very much one of the smooth absorption of immigrants and the overcoming of the cultural and linguistic handicaps of belonging to immigrant communities (Verma with Ashworth, 1986). But it was also an expression of concern about the potential hampering of the progress of white pupils in multi-racial classes. As the Swann Report (*op. cit.*) observes, whatever problems this policy may have caused for individual ethnic minority pupils, it certainly went a long way in confirming among the wider white population the view that immigrant children in general were essentially an educational problem and a threat to the well-being of indigenous children.

Whether it was because of philosophical dissatisfaction with the assimilationist model or a more pragmatic response to its apparent failure, school responses moved towards a more integrationist approach. The focus was still on the needs of the ethnic minorities and the expectation largely was that they should adapt, the emphasis being, in the then HMI Eric Bolton's words, 'upon integrating the minorities with the majority society and culture so that a culturally homogeneous society would be created' (Bolton, 1979). As early as 1966, the then Home Secretary Roy Jenkins had argued that the national goal should be seen as 'not a flattening process of assimilation but as equal opportunity accompanied by cultural diversity in an atmosphere of mutual tolerance', thus implying that perhaps mainstream society had some adaptive role to play in this too. By 1971, the DES was speaking more about creating a harmonious society rather than just meeting the needs of immigrants. As the DES Circular on the Education of Immigrants put it:

> Schools can demonstrate how people from different ethnic groups and cultural backgrounds can live together happily and successfully, and can help to create the kind of cohesive, multi-cultural society on which the future of this country — and possibly the world — depends (DES, 1971).

However, Verma and Bagley's (1984) research findings in the mid 1970s demonstrated that the education of minority children was still largely 'problem orientated'. Referring back to this period, the Swann Report (*op. cit.*) argued that:

> in practice there was little real difference between the assimilationist and integrationist viewpoints in that they shared the common aim of absorbing ethnic minority communities within society with as little disruption to the life of the majority community as possible.

Mullard (1982) goes further in identifying subtle forces in the integrationist approach to ensure assimilation and social control.

> The political imperative of assimilation in this model is no longer, as constructed in the early 1960s, dependent upon complete cultural subjugation: the means to the ends have slightly changed, but the ends remain the same.

The third stage in this development is usually described as 'pluralism'. The Swann Report (*op. cit.*) identified 'pluralism' as the model of society which should inform and direct future educational policies and practices:

> We consider that a multi-racial society such as ours would in fact function most effectively and harmoniously on the basis of pluralism which enables, expects and encourages members of all ethnic groups, both minority and majority, to participate fully in shaping the society as a whole within a framework of commonly accepted values, practices and procedures while also allowing and, where necessary, assisting the ethnic minority communities in maintaining their distinct ethnic identities within this common framework (DES, 1985).

While this is not the place for a full discussion of pluralism, it is important to recognise that there is no single model of plural societies, and discussions about the implications of pluralism often raise more fundamental issues of social theory and ideology (see, for example, Jeffcoate, 1984; Mullard, 1984; Lynch, 1989). The discussion by Zec of cultural relativism (1981) and the papers presented to the CRE 1989 Seminar on Pluralism (CRE, 1990), illustrate the complex issues associated with developing philosophical models of pluralism and practical responses which might be appropriate in Britain.

Verma (1990), for example, argues that at the moment British society is in a state of disequilibrium. The ethnic minority groups in its midst find themselves in large part marginalised by dominant groups, who, in turn, have yet to recognise the ways in which their actions and behaviours (whether intentional or unintentional) and their cultural assumptions contribute to that marginalisation. Furthermore:

> Unless we match up to this responsibility, we run the risk of, at best, a pluralism that lacks cohesion and under which ethnic minority groups are forced to look increasingly inwards, because they find themselves excluded from a viable existence within mainstream society. The type of pluralist society for which we must strive is one that stresses core values but allows for diversity within an agreed framework.

Despite being described as 'a landmark in pluralism' (Verma, 1989), the Swann Report came under attack from several sources for its concept of pluralism in the British context. Two responses, one from a Muslim perspective and the other from a Marxist critique, illustrate the problems which arise when the concept of pluralism is interpreted quite differently. In an agreed statement, a number of Muslim groups in Britain challenged the 'integrational pluralism' adopted by Swann, preferring a 'dynamic pluralism' by which the Muslim community would 'preserve all elements of its culture and lifestyle which are ultimately derived from the Qur'an and the Sunnah, and reinforced through the educational curricula that would acknowledge and allow those basic values of Islam to be preserved' (Islamic Academy, 1985). Mullard (1985), on the other hand, in a paper presented to a conference on the Swann Report at Bradford University argued that Swann used the term 'pluralist' in a purely descriptive way, failing to acknowledge that for all practical purposes Britain is not a plural but a class-based society. He went on to argue that:

> We can dismiss the pluralism because whenever an issue appears in the Report which basically raises the issue of pluralism, the committee comes out against it as, for example, in the separate schools debate . . . Immediately the issue of plurality or pluralism appears the committee comes back with an assimilationist pitch and basically a class analysis of society (Mullard, 1985).

While the Swann Report's somewhat imprecise use of the concept of pluralism may have provided a useful peg for further development in educational response, unless a more precise understanding of the sense in which Britain wishes to commit itself to pluralism is agreed, 'pluralist' is likely to be little more than the latest synonym for 'multi-cultural'.

Multi-cultural Education

The broad school response to this developing pattern has been widely described as 'multi-cultural education', although the term has been, and continues to be, subject to a wide range of interpretations. The development of multi-cultural education reflected a change of emphasis from earlier assimilationist approaches. In the words of the Swann Report:

> The most obvious difference between the early days of assimilation and integration, and the concept of multi-cultural education is that, whereas the former focused primarily on seeking to 'remedy' the perceived 'problems' of ethnic minority children and to compensate for their perceived 'disabilities', multi-cultural education has usually tended to have two distinct themes — firstly, meeting the particular educational needs of ethnic minority children and secondly, the broader issue of preparing *all* pupils for life in a multi-racial society (DES, 1985).

Multi-cultural responses to education have been attacked on a number of fronts. Rex (1989) has argued that the effect of multi-culturalism, unless coupled with a clear equality of opportunity philosophy, is to divide society and further penalise ethnic minorities. Mullard (1982) concludes that multi-cultural education, as promoted by many LEAs, has been used more as an instrument of social control than as a genuine means of promoting pluralism. Early attempts at 'multi-racial' education and the introduction of black studies have been dismissed by Stone (1981) as compensatory education based on false models of self-esteem and more concerned with satisfying the conscience of teachers than meeting the real needs of pupils. Perhaps the most widespread criticism has been directed at the focus on the cultures of minorities rather than the racism of the dominant community (e.g. Lynch, 1987).

Multi-cultural education is at best an extremely imprecise concept. It has grown largely out of a liberal reaction to earlier assimilationist models. Inevitably, as Jeffcoate (1984a) has argued, those who hold to reactionary or radical ideologies are likely to be suspicious, if not dismissive, of the whole movement. However, as a broad and largely unthreatening description of attempts within education, particularly at classroom level, to take seriously the multi-ethnic nature of British society, the concept of 'multi-cultural education' has provided a useful rallying standard.

The more recent 'anti-racist education' movement has been described as both a development of multi-cultural education and a reaction against it. The way in which NAME was able to retain its acronym while changing its title from the National Association for Multi-racial Education to the National Anti-racist Movement in Education perhaps illustrates the change of emphasis many educationists adopted in the late 1980s. It grew out of a realisation that simply focusing on cultural diversity did not ensure that more subtle forms of racism, particularly at an institutional level, would be addressed. Central to the concept of anti-racist education is the need to deal with racial discrimination and to develop a more critical approach to all teaching methods and materials. As Rex (1989) puts it, 'anti-racism has a moral purpose going beyond multi-cultural education'.

However, for others, anti-racist education has been seen as the antithesis of multi-cultural education. Mullard (1984) traces its origins to the Black Consciousness Movement of the mid-1960s. He goes on to argue that:

> The contest between and debate around anti-racist and multicultural education is far more fundamental than is often supposed. It is not just a question of alternatives . . . Nor is it merely a contested space in which a dynamic and political process can be developed . . . But instead the debate reflects and encompasses oppositional definitions of socio-educational reality.

Attempts to 'bridge the gulf' between anti-racist and multi-cultural models by Grinter (1985) and others produced a concept of 'anti-racist multi-culturalism'. In his later writing, Grinter argues that the gulf is unbridgeable and 'the philosophies do not meet' (Grinter, 1990). In practice, as Grinter argues, terminology is perhaps less important than the practical responses of teachers.

It would be simplistic to suggest that these models or practical responses to pluralism follow a linear historical development. All the concepts outlined above can still be found to some degree in schools. Since some uses of the terms described reflect deeper political or ideological positions, they are likely to continue to be debated. Rex (1989), for example, sees the three continuing key issues to be equality of opportunity, multi-culturalism and anti-racism. Indeed, many schools are currently seeking to include their response to cultural diversity or racism with an over-arching policy of equal opportunities which combines issues of race, gender, class and disability.

The Education Reform Act, 1988

By the late 1980s, preoccupation with the demands of the Education Reform Act and the National Curriculum had diverted much attention and energy away from programmes of multi-cultural or anti-racist education. As this present study shows, teachers' answers to questions about developing multi-cultural policies or curriculum responses frequently refer to the pressures of the national curriculum or other recent educational innovations preventing them giving such matters the attention they deserve. Grinter (1990) argues that 'the 1986–88 educational legislation initiates structural changes that are potentially very damaging to the prospects for anti-racist education'. Certainly, an in-depth analysis of the curriculum suggests that minority cultures *have* been neglected in the development of the core and foundation subjects. Many minority children and young people are presented with an

Anglocentric curriculum which is not only alien and exclusive, but which obliterates the realities of their ethnic identities and experiences (Verma, 1992).

The introduction of the National Curriculum was an excellent opportunity to recognise differences in terms of ethnicity and culture in our society. In so doing it would not only have reassured minority pupils of the value given to their cultures but would have helped to prepare all children for the realities of life in Britain's plural society. In the event, we have, as Verma (1992) observes, a curriculum which eliminates cultural differences 'not by denying the values, beliefs and customs of other cultures but by assuming that they do not even exist!' The controversy lies not so much in the broad explicit goals of the National Curriculum — which do allow for pluralist and equal opportunities responses (even if only as an afterthought) — but with the detailed statements on content and purpose within individual subject areas and methods of assessment. It is still too early to determine the long-term impact of the centralised control of the curriculum on schools. However, the opportunity presented by the 1988 Education Reform Act for the government to make a clear and unequivocal commitment to multi-cultural education was clearly not grasped.

This failure to embrace a more international or pluralist approach to the National Curriculum was also reflected in the government's requirements for religious education and school worship. The clumsy way in which the RE clauses in the Act were written and presented led many members of religious minorities to believe that, at best, their faith was being devalued and, at worst, their children would be inducted into Christianity (Sarwar, 1988). Subsequent debate and clarification have helped to alleviate such fears but there remains a widespread concern which, while not denying the weaknesses of some world faiths' approaches, anticipates the loss of the benefits gained in helping children and young people to understand something of each other's faith. Much now depends on the extent to which the national guidelines for local agreed syllabuses reflect professional and community concern that all faiths are given due respect (Hull, 1993). While it is important that all children learn about Christianity and its contributions to the life and history of Britain, this should not be allowed to degenerate into a nationalistic approach to a faith which, from a world perspective, has more black than white adherents and even in Britain finds its strongest growing points among the black churches. Equally important is whether the model of RE promoted includes a genuine attempt to help all pupils to understand about the religious pluralism of Britain and to develop skills to cope with the diversity of commitments and practices to be found both between, and within, religious communities.

The issue of school worship has proved even more contentious. Early Muslim responses to the worship clauses in the Act led to many requests for pupils to be withdrawn from school assembly. Sensitive negotiations by schools often avoided unwelcome divisiveness but headteachers have expressed continuing concern about the inappropriateness of some of the Act's expectations (NAHT, 1989). In our experience, many schools feel obliged to adopt approaches to school assembly more in keeping with the communities they serve rather than simply keeping the letter of the law.

Racism and Schools

Two driving forces have motivated the educational response to plural Britain: first, the initial desire to assimilate or integrate ethnic minorities; second, the increasing concern about ethnic minority apparent underachievement. Although the Swann Report explored a wide range of issues, its original brief was to explore whether ethnic minority children, particularly West Indians, were underachieving within the education system and, if so, what factors contributed to this underachievement. However, a third force, that of racism, has consistently emerged as a power in education which cannot be ignored.

In 1973 the Parliamentary Select Committee on Race Relations and Immigration recommended 'unity through diversity' in schools and called for a government programme which focused on race (Select Committee, 1973). The then Secretary of State's response, *Educational Disadvantage and the Educational Needs of Immigrants* (DES, 1974) rejected the suggestion, identifying the appropriate response in terms of the educational needs of all disadvantaged children. As Kirp (1979) observes, 'the DES constantly preferred almost any identifying label — "non-English speaking", "culturally deprived", "educationally disadvantaged" — to the racial one'.

Unconscious racism was identified by the Rampton Report (DES, 1981) as part of the complex pattern of factors which had brought about West Indian underachievement. The Swann Report (DES, 1985) went further, devoting a major theoretical chapter to issues of racism in education. What research evidence exists is partial and unclear. The CRE report, *Learning in Terror*, argued that schools were one of the places where ethnic minority pupils were having to endure:

> the insecurity and anxiety arising from the threatening atmosphere associated with the possibility of racial insults, graffiti and violence directed at them, their families and communities (CRE, 1988).

The murder of Ahmed Ullah at Burnage School, Manchester in 1986 opened up a wide and often acrimonious debate. When the full investigation of the school was eventually published (MacDonald, 1989) it revealed that pupils and teachers had suffered from a range of racist abuse and attacks. Generalisations from one school are inappropriate. Smith and Tomlinson's (1989) major investigation of school effectiveness found 'no evidence that racial hostility at school is an important factor for 12 and 13-year-old children' and that parents 'rarely mentioned racial prejudice or hostility of any kind'. As the authors point out, what is really lacking is hard evidence of the size and extent of any racial problems which might exist. Troyna (1991) has argued that the failure to obtain such hard evidence is due, at least in part, to the very research methodologies employed (see our discussion in Chapter 2).

Racism can take a variety of forms. It can be personal and direct, as in the case of racist name-calling. It can be social and discriminatory against whole groups. It can be institutional, hampering in perhaps the most insidious way, the life chances of black pupils. The Rampton and Swann reports argued that there are also forms of racism which are best described as 'unintentional'. Whatever form racism might take, the Swann Report was unequivocal in its belief that the function of schools is to tackle it.

> If in the face of such forms of racism, or indeed in the face of ignorance and inaccurate statements about ethnic minorities, the school seeks simply to remain neutral and uninvolved we would see this as not only a failure in terms of its educational responsibilities but also as in effect condoning and thereby encouraging the persistence of such occurrences. Certainly it is difficult for ethnic minority communities to have full confidence and trust in an institution which they see as simply ignoring or dismissing what is in fact an ever-present and all-pervasive shadow over their everyday lives (DES, 1985, p. 35).

This chapter has demonstrated the range of complex factors which impinge directly or indirectly on the lives and education of all pupils in British schools. Evidence about the quality of inter-ethnic relationships in schools is scarce and inconclusive. Theories about appropriate educational responses to pluralism continue to be developed and debated. School responses have been diverse and inconsistent and often dependent on local (or even individual) initiatives rather than central government guidelines and support.

There is clearly a continuing need for systematic study of the effectiveness of schools in preparing all students for life in plural Britain. The present study took as its main focus multi-ethnic schools and the nature of student relationships in them. In the following chapter we describe the research strategy adopted.

Chapter 2

Inter-Ethnic Relationships: The Conduct of the Research

The first intensive field studies in British educational institutions took place in the 1960s. During the following decade, schools (and particularly classrooms) became a focus for systematic, ethnographic and socio-linguistic studies opening up a wide debate over the appropriate use of research methods in education, not least the relative merits of qualitative and quantitative approaches (Hargreaves, 1980).

Recent in-depth comparative studies of schools have been greatly influenced by Rutter's (1979) pioneering study *Fifteen Thousand Hours*, the prime focus of which was to study the broad patterns of life in schools and the 'kinds of environments for learning which they present to their pupils'. Later studies which drew on the style and findings of Rutter's study include *School Matters* (Mortimore, 1988) — ILEA's study of junior schools — and *The School Effect*, Smith and Tomlinson's (1989) study of twenty multi-racial comprehensives. These studies were essentially quantitative, drawing on longitudinal data and sophisticated analytical techniques to measure differences between schools. Studies of a more qualitative nature include Woods' (1979) *The Divided School* and Foster's (1990) *Policy and Practice in Multi-cultural and Anti-racist Education*. Both pieces of research involved detailed study of just one secondary school.

Woods, drawing on the symbolic interactionist tradition in which human activity is understood in terms of the meanings objects and events have for the individuals involved in the process of social interaction, sought to study and portray the broad patterns of school life in the context of wider society. Foster's prime concern was to follow up initial interview and survey work conducted by the ESRC Research Unit on Ethnic Relations by 'examining in more detail how schools and individual teachers responded to LEA policies on multi-cultural education, and what the effects of these policies actually were at school level' (Foster, 1990). A single, multi-ethnic secondary school was chosen and an ethnographic study, not unlike that of Woods above, was conducted. However, in addition to the taking of field notes, the researcher conducted interviews, 'some structured, others less so' with staff and students, and examined a large number of school documents.

In none of these studies was inter-ethnic *relationships* the central focus of the research, although *The School Effect* (Smith and Tomlinson, 1989) did include as one of its objectives 'to describe the educational experience of children belonging to racial minority groups' and Foster's study included discussions with pupils about the nature and extent of racism in school. However, since the 1960s there has been a steady flow of often relatively small-scale research into friendship patterns in multi-racial schools drawing on a range of instruments including questionnaires, interviews and pupil responses to black and white dolls. Similarly, there has been a small number of studies investigating positive and negative *factors* influencing such friendship patterns including the impact of school structures, self-image, black/white ratios, and language. The establishing of the Rampton/Swann Committee (DES, 1981; 1985) provided new impetus for research into the experiences of ethnic minority pupils in school. During the 1980s, and particularly since the publication of the Swann Report in 1985, a number of studies have been conducted directly into 'race relations' in schools. Among these were Spencer's (1987) survey of 500 pupils in the London Borough of Barnet, The Commission for Racial Equality's (1988) survey of racial harassment in schools and colleges, Kelly's (1989) enquiry into race relations in Manchester schools commissioned by the Macdonald enquiry into the murder of Ahmed Ullah, and the Newham Study (1990) of *Racism and Racist Violence in Schools*. These studies were essentially surveys based on first hand reports, discussions and questionnaires. As Kelly concludes:

> The survey of students undertaken in the three Manchester schools should be viewed as a 'trawl by questionnaire' which has thrown up indicators and clues which need to be pursued if students, teachers and parents are to clarify the ways in which racial differences are filtering their way through schools (*ibid.*).

During the period of our research, several small-scale studies have been conducted into aspects of inter-ethnic relationships in schools. These include a questionnaire-based study of the experience of bullying by thirty-three matched pairs of Asian and white pupils (Moran *et al.*, 1993), Wright's (1992) ethnographic study of six primary schools and Gillborn's (1990) examination of day-to-day interaction, conflict and negotiation between teachers and pupils of different ethnic groups. However, we believe that the 'indicators and clues' identified by Kelly are still not being pursued in any systematic way by researchers. The issue is not simply a matter of gathering more statistical data. We agree with Troyna's (1991) reservations about both case study and more quantitative types of empirical research, given the complexity of this field. Of the 'case study' approach taken by a number of enquiries into racial harassment in schools, he says:

> . . . (they) have collated an impressive range of evidence to demonstrate the tenacity and pervasiveness of 'racial' incidents in schools.

He contrasts that approach with

> . . . more formal, quantitative methods of analysing racial harassment. . . . A statistical profile of 'racial' incidents in schools has been built on student responses to questionnaires, word and sentence completion tests, structured classroom observation and interviews with students, parents and

teachers. Interestingly, and in contrast to the general conclusions drawn from more discursive studies of this issue, quantitative researchers have been more circumspect about the prevalence of 'racial' incidents in schools.

Troyna acknowledges that 'anecdotal' evidence from case studies about 'racial' incidents in schools is often too imprecise and partial to be an adequate basis for generalisation, policy development and professional practice. But his critique of Kelly's (1990) study of racial name-calling in Manchester secondary schools, and of Smith and Tomlinson's (1989) *The School Effect* argues converse weaknesses in a 'supposedly more systematic' approach. Both Kelly, and Smith and Tomlinson, report that overt racism is not on the whole a large-scale problem in multi-ethnic schools, or at any rate in those studied by them (three in Kelly's case, twenty in Smith and Tomlinson's). But the approach taken by these researchers is, Troyna believes, open to three main criticisms. First, the apparent absence of 'overt racism' does not necessarily negate claims about the prevalence or seriousness of racist behaviour. Second, in relying on others', especially parents', perceptions of children's experiences in school, rather than on students' reports of their own experiences couched in their own language, such enquiries are likely to miss the 'subtle and complex nature of racism in education' through failing to register the narrative of the main actors. Third, studies of the Smith and Tomlinson type tend to concentrate on 'assembling statistical data on the observable, detectable and therefore easily measurable forms of racism.' As such, they may be influential in areas of policy and programmes of action, but may also 'sacrifice understanding . . . on the altar of description'.

We believe that Troyna is right in arguing that surveys, even those as sophisticated as used by Smith and Tomlinson, are too crude to capture the subtle and complex nature of racism in education. Although our discussion throughout this book clearly indicates that we believe in the value of quantitative methods (our survey of more than 2,000 students provided valuable data about the general patterns of students' views and experiences in multi-ethnic schools), our concern has been to go beyond the 'what' of students' experiences to the 'how' and 'why'. Furthermore, we were eager to hear not just what teachers or parents believed to be the experiences of students but to hear from students themselves. As Gilborn and Drew (1992) have demonstrated in the case of *The School Effect*'s conclusions about racism in schools, it is all too easy to accept the *absence of evidence* of racism in the testimony of parents and teachers, *as evidence of the absence* of racism in the lives of students.

In deciding at the start to employ a 'mixed-method' research approach, embodied in multi-site case studies, we were aiming essentially to do three things: first, penetrating school students' and teachers' experience of inter-ethnic relationships through recording what they would tell us; second, implementing that procedure across nine very roughly similar institutions, with the anticipated (and realised) outcomes of both illuminating variety and some suggestive patterning; third, exploiting the number of institutional case studies to carry out a quantitative analysis based on a large (2,300) student sample.

Four main perspectives on inter-ethnic relationships shaped our study of each school: the experiences and perceptions of staff; the experiences and perceptions of students; the formal position of the school as represented by official documents; and the observations of the researcher while in school. Research instruments were designed to gather data in all these areas. There are clear advantages in the use of a variety of research methods alongside each other. Such 'triangulation' not only helps to generate the different kinds of data essential to producing a portrait of each school but greatly increases the chances of accuracy. Triangular techniques:

> attempt to map out, or explain more fully, the richness and complexity of human behaviour by studying it from more than one standpoint and, in so doing, by making use of both quantitative and qualitative data (Cohen and Manion, 1989).

Our study generated a very large amount of ethnographic data, against a substantial backdrop of statistical material. The latter, however, is not entirely of the sort criticised for its limitations by Troyna. The questionnaire (see Appendix 3, p. 141) was administered exclusively to the whole Year 8 and Year 10 student cohorts from which the interviewees were taken and its questions followed closely the subject-matter of the interview schedules (see Appendix 2, p. 134). There is, therefore, a relationship between the qualitative and quantitative data, and that this is so is borne out in later chapters of this book. It is readily acknowledged that that relationship could well be further explored. We are convinced that, although this study has proved more complex than would have been the case had either approach been used on its own, the interaction between the two has been fruitful.

Criteria of Selection of Schools

Within the limits of time available, and in order to allow for a reasonable depth of study in each school, it was decided to aim for a sample of ten schools. Constraints on time and access reduced the final sample size to nine. As Smith and Tomlinson (1989) observe, there is great difficulty in 'matching' schools in a sample of this kind. Such matching is more critical when comparability is a central objective of the research. For a case study approach it is not only less critical but to a certain extent undesirable. Too much homogeneity reduces the opportunities to observe a full range of contributory factors. However, the reduction of some variables in the sample schools does allow for the use of identical research instruments and for the emergence of patterns and contrasts.

The nature of the research required that all schools in the sample should include among their students some children from ethnic minority backgrounds. To ensure a reasonable degree of ethnic mix in the sample schools, only those with a minimum of 25 per cent ethnic minority students were considered. In addition, all schools chosen had (officially, at least) comprehensive intakes and were mixed by gender.

Access to schools involves extensive negotiation. An independent investigation of an area as sensitive as inter-ethnic relationships is likely to be welcomed only by local education authorities and individual schools which are reasonably confident that they are at least 'on the right tracks'. As Smith and Tomlinson discovered, securing agreement by local education authorities to take part in such studies and maintaining teacher cooperation is not easy, particularly when many in education feel that 'a research project that is explicitly concerned with distinct ethnic groups is digging up something that they would prefer to remain buried' (*op. cit.*). There was therefore no suggestion of taking a random sample of either LEAs or schools. LEA advisers were asked to identify schools which they felt were at least seeking to respond to the challenge of educating for ethnic diversity. Headteachers at these schools were then approached and discussions were held, often involving other senior teachers and in some cases the whole staff.

The final sample of nine schools was drawn from six local authorities, two in the south of England and four in the north-west. The proportion of their students from ethnic minority backgrounds varied from 25 per cent to 75 per cent. In order to preserve anonymity we have given each of the schools which participated in the study the name of a tree and these names are used throughout this book.

Suitable times for visiting school and procedures for gathering data were negotiated with each school. A request was made that if all staff were not involved in the initial negotiations then an early opportunity was presented for the researcher to meet them. In this way everyone was made aware of the investigation and all teachers were encouraged to see themselves as contributing to the research. Although some schools offered the use of some sort of 'base' (including, on one occasion, the headteacher's office) for the researchers, the staff room usually emerged as the most suitable place for establishing and developing relationships with staff which, although time-consuming, are the key to effective research. Formal interviews, on the other hand, were always conducted in private.

Nine schools were visited by members of the research team. The equivalent of half a term was spent in each school and opportunities were taken to observe students in a variety of situations, to talk formally and informally with staff and students and to gather general data about school life as opportunities arose. Semi-structured interviews were conducted with a total of 281 year 8 and year 10 students and with 190 teachers (including headteachers). A total of 2,326 questionnaires were completed by year 8 and year 10 students.

The Five Northern Schools

In terms of the ethnicity of students, the five northern schools fell into two categories. Three schools (Elm School, Pine School and Birch School) were essentially 'bi-cultural' and 'bi-lingual' and were typical of many schools in smaller industrial 'mill' towns where for historical reasons ethnic minority families are drawn largely from one community. However, in each of these schools there were also some students from other minority backgrounds. The other two schools (Ash School and Yew School) were city centre schools and more accurately described as multi-racial and multi-lingual.

Elm School was a mixed secondary school serving what was once a small industrial town on the east side of Manchester. The school was formed from the amalgamation of three schools in 1986. There were seventy teachers in the school, two of whom were from Afro-Caribbean backgrounds. There were no Asian teachers, although Bengali speaking 'Section 11' support staff were present in school. *Pine School* was a large mixed secondary school close to the centre of a small industrial town. The town's Bangladeshi community of almost 4,000 was already the third largest in Britain and growing rapidly. The community displayed a very young age profile with almost 61 per cent under the age of 16 (compared with 20 per cent of the overall population). The majority of this community arrived in the ten years preceding the research. *Birch School* was a mixed secondary school on the edge of a northern 'cotton town' with a population of almost a quarter of a million people. Of these, some 25,000 were from ethnic minority backgrounds, mainly Gujerati (both Muslim and Hindu) with a smaller proportion of families from Pakistani backgrounds. The communities closest to the school were predominantly Pakistani and Gujerati Muslims. *Ash School* and *Yew School*, unlike the three schools described above, had students from a greater variety of ethnic backgrounds. Both schools were close to the centre of a large city. However, there were some significant differences between the two schools. Ash School had been amalgamated from two schools and at the time of the research still functioned on two bases, a mile apart. Yew School was a recently formed aided school with a relatively modern (or modernised) building. Although a Church of England school, it had grown out of both ecumenical and inter-faith dialogue and had a commitment to take students from a wide range of ethnic and religious backgrounds built into its foundation charter.

The Four Southern Schools

Beech School was a 11–18 comprehensive school situated in an inner city area of London. Although the school drew students from a wide area, its immediate catchment area was mainly working class and had become increasingly ethnically diverse in recent years, the most recent group to arrive being Bangladeshi. The school did not have precise details of the ethnic breakdown of its 690 students, but estimates indicated that approximately 50 per cent of students were from Bangladeshi backgrounds. *Fir School* was a large comprehensive school of 1,100 students situated in a predominantly white middle-class suburb of Greater London. The housing in the area was a mixture of affluent owner-occupied properties and council estates. Although, according to the headteacher, the school catered for 'the full social-economic range' of families, most students came from 'middle-class' backgrounds. The school did not keep precise details of the ethnic background of students and staff perceptions of the range and degree of cultural diversity in school varied significantly. However, according to the headteacher's approximation, 40 per cent of students came from ethnic minority backgrounds, the largest group being Cypriot (mainly Greek rather than Turkish). *Larch School* was a co-educational 11–18 comprehensive school situated in a working-class residential area of north London.

At the time of the research the school had 997 students on roll and a teaching staff of 74. The school did not keep records of the ethnicity of its staff or students. According to the headteacher, a third of the students were 'white indigenous', a third were Afro-Caribbean and a third comprised 'non-English speakers' — Kurds, Somalis and Bengalis. This latter third was increasing (from six to forty in the two years preceding the research). *Oak School* described itself as a 'mixed, international comprehensive school'. It was situated in the north-west district of London. The school was thirty years old and had an eight-form entry with a total of 1,200 students. The school did not keep records of the ethnicity of its students and estimates were made difficult by the large number of students from mixed backgrounds. However, the overall percentage of bilingual Commonwealth and non-Commonwealth students was estimated at 37 per cent of the total school roll, with an additional 20 per cent from Afro-Caribbean backgrounds. In addition, twenty-six students from refugee groups were present in school.

The Research Instruments

In addition to the gathering and analysis of documents published in and by the schools, four main research techniques were used: individual interviews, structured group discussions, a student questionnaire and researcher observations.

Interviews with Staff

It was clear from the outset that the perceptions and experiences of staff would be central to any understanding of the state of inter-ethnic relationships in the schools and the procedures being adopted to promote good relationships. While it would have been possible to circulate all staff in each school with a questionnaire, the sensitive and complex nature of the issues being explored really demanded an approach which allowed for more freedom to explore issues in depth. Although it meant reducing the size of the sample, individual interviews were chosen as the most appropriate method. Schools are extremely complex areas of social interaction and there may be social processes taking place of which teachers are unaware. It is possible, however, for a researcher to increase teachers' awareness by revealing such processes and patterns of interaction.

Interviewing styles vary from the highly structured (useful when seeking answers to a large number of relatively simple questions) to the totally unstructured 'depth' interviews (often associated with psychotherapy). The need in this research to allow respondents to express themselves freely (and, occasionally, at length) while maintaining the general direction and shape of the enquiry, suggested that a semi-structured approach would be most appropriate. The focus of the research was on inter-ethnic relationships and teachers were asked to comment on the quality of inter-student relationships and to give examples from their own experience of positive and negative inter-ethnic encounters in school, including the extent to which students from different ethnic backgrounds mixed. In addition, questions were asked about teachers' background and training, their views about the impact of school policy and practice on student relationships and the wider links the school had with local communities. At the end of interviews, teachers were invited to offer additional observations about inter-ethnic relationships in general or the particular circumstances of the school.

As with all the instruments used in the research, the final form of the interview schedule emerged from studies in two pilot schools. These schools were used not merely for testing instruments but as an essential stage in the design of the research. Formal and informal discussions with teachers helped to identify a series of key issues which were then incorporated into a semi-structured interview schedule. This schedule was tested with teachers to determine the length of time required for each interview, the natural flow of the topics to be covered and any problems of language and understanding. The schedule was designed to progress naturally through the areas being investigated while allowing teachers (or the researcher) to divert to some other topic if appropriate. Analysis of the data generated by the pilot schedules led to further modifications, in particular the inclusion of spaces for the interviewer to make brief notes during the interview on the schedule, and even to code some responses where questions were relatively simple or factual. This latter provision proved to be important in coping with the limitations of time at the formal analytical stage of the research.

At the end of the pilot stage, teachers were asked to complete a short anonymous questionnaire expressing their views and feelings about the process of being interviewed. The vast majority of comments were positive and most teachers appeared to welcome the experience. Comments about the process of setting up interviews and approaching teachers (for example, the personal negotiation of appropriate times for conducting interviews rather than relying on appointments made by senior staff) were taken into account in the procedures adopted in the main study.

Limitations on time meant that not all teachers in each school could be interviewed. In addition, the researchers were entirely dependent on the cooperation of staff and had no power to commandeer teachers for interviews. Bearing in mind these constraints, the following teachers were identified as key members for the sample:

- firstly, all senior staff: they would have the ultimate responsibility for the implementation of the school's policy and practice and would have the widest overall perception of inter-ethnic relationships in school (for example, through dealing with discipline matters);
- secondly, any teacher with oversight of the school's multi-cultural/anti-racist education policy;
- thirdly, all ethnic minority teachers (if at all possible): it is perhaps worth noting at this stage that we initially had in mind those teachers from black or Asian backgrounds; during the research, a number of other teachers from, for example, Irish, Welsh and Ukrainian backgrounds were also chosen for interview (using other criteria) and contributed particularly interesting comments on the position of teachers and students from less 'obvious' minority communities;

- fourthly, as many heads of departments (and/or faculties) as possible: this would provide useful data about the function of the curriculum in influencing inter-ethnic relationships;
- finally, teachers who in informal conversations appeared to have particular insights or experiences which would help us to gain a clearer picture of the school: wherever possible, at least one recently appointed teacher was interviewed in order to give a newcomer's perspective.

The above sampling procedure was generally followed in all nine schools. However, pressures from time-tabling, absenteeism as well as the general high administrative expectations placed on teachers at present, meant that in none of the schools was it possible to adhere strictly to this sample. A very small proportion of teachers approached declined to be interviewed. However, in each school, a minimum of 25 per cent of all staff were interviewed, including all senior teachers and all ethnic minority teachers. The final semi-structured interview schedule for teachers is included as Appendix 1 (p. 125).

In addition to the formal interviews outlined above, opportunities were taken to talk to staff informally whenever possible. Comments and experiences were recorded on simple data recording sheets as soon as possible after conversations had taken place and these records provided additional valuable data about staff perceptions of the school in general and inter-ethnic relationships in particular.

Interviews with Students

Gathering data from students about their experiences of inter-ethnic relationships and their views about school policy and practice proved more complex. Researchers have often reported the reluctance of students to respond in asymmetrical interview situations and a tendency to resort to defensive, monosyllabic behaviour. However, for the same reasons outlined above, it was felt that a semi-structured interview approach, supplemented with informal conversations and small group discussions, would produce the most accurate and revealing data. A semi-structured schedule (see Appendix 2) was designed in order to gather specific data about experiences and attitudes while allowing freedom to explore issues seen as important by the interviewee. The areas covered were similar to those developed for the teachers so that comparisons could be made between the perceptions of teachers and those of students'.

The limitations of time meant that it was impossible to interview students in all age groups. It was decided to exclude year 7 students on the grounds that their experience of the school (particularly if research was taking place in the autumn term) would be limited. Similarly, year 11 students were excluded on practical grounds because of the difficulties produced by open timetabling and examinations during the spring and summer terms. In order to provide a reasonable range of ages, it was decided to focus on year 8 and year 10 students.

Having chosen the age groups, a number of sampling procedures were explored. Consideration was given to identifying ethnic groups in school and selecting representatives from each group. But, as Bullivant (1987) observes, the factors which make for ethnic identity, especially ethnic self-identity, are complex and make it difficult to select children from pre-defined ethnic backgrounds for research purposes. Eventually, it was decided to adopt a simple systematic sampling procedure, interviewing 10 per cent of all students in year 8 and year 10. In practice, even 10 per cent proved too large a sample to complete, and a final sample of one in twelve was used. Students were chosen from the year lists by starting with a random number between one and twelve and then including every twelfth student.

Questionnaire

A questionnaire (Appendix 3) was designed to gather a large quantity of data from students in order to provide a broader backcloth to the research findings. Nearly all year 8 and year 10 students completed the questionnaire, which consisted mainly of multiple choice questions with a four or five point scale. Where appropriate, open ended questions or options were included but these were kept to a minimum in order to facilitate coding and analysis of completed questionnaires. Students were asked to identify communities, religious and language groups to which they felt they belonged and to indicate their experience of positive and negative relationships in school, including experiences of bullying and name-calling. For some schools in the sample, bilingual (English and Bengali, English and Turkish) versions were provided after discussion with year heads and section 11 staff.

It is clear that the size of the questionnaire sample, and the very large number of possible variables and combinations of variables embedded in it, justified a lot more analysis than the time and resources available to this study were able to yield. It was indeed possible to undertake *some* analysis which went beyond crude whole-sample frequency and which yielded some striking information. Nevertheless, the interaction between evidence from surveys and from interviews and observation was valuable: in particular, as we shall bring out in later chapters, it enabled us to discern patterns within and between schools in perceptions of the quality of inter-ethnic relationships and to tease out possible factors underlying those patterns. To give one example here: differences emerged in the questionnaire results between the perceived quality of relationships, as seen by all students on the one hand and by Muslims on the other. That finding was much enriched by interviews with students and teachers.

In addition, several small group discussions were arranged with year 8 and year 10 students and these provided both additional data about student experiences and perceptions as well as some valuable insights into the dynamics of student relationships in the groups.

As with the staff interview schedule, research instruments for use with students were developed through work in the pilot schools. The semi-structured interview schedule was modified as a result of a series of interviews with pilot school students. Important modifications to a preliminary questionnaire were made as a result of discussions held with students who had completed it in the pilot schools.

Additional Information

General information about each school and, in particular, its policy with regard to equal opportunities and ethnic diversity, was obtained from published school documents. These included the school prospectus, policy statements, staff handbooks, curriculum policy statements and newsletters.

General impressions of the schools were built up through recorded observations in various formal and informal situations in school, including observation in the yard, in the dining hall(s), in selected lessons and at school functions. A diary of observations and conversations was kept. Structured data recording sheets, which had been developed in the pilot schools, helped to speed up recording and to maintain the focus of the research during the writing of field notes. The research team reflected a variety of ethnic and religious backgrounds, and included both sexes. In all schools, observation and some interviews were conducted by someone other than the main researcher as a check against researcher bias.

At the design stage of the research, consideration was given to systematic observation in class using time sampling and coding techniques based on methods developed by the ORACLE Project (Galton *et al.*, 1980) in order to obtain quantitative data about inter-ethnic interactions during lessons. Although the system appeared to have some potential, results from piloting the instruments indicated that the amount of time needed to be given over to classroom observation in order to produce reliable data would be unrealistic in a research programme of this scale.

Using the instruments described above, a large quantity of rich data was obtained. Detailed semi-structured interviews were conducted with almost 200 teachers and almost 300 students. Several hundred hours were spent in observation and informal conversations. Questionnaires were completed by more than 2,300 students. A wide range of documentary evidence was collected from schools and LEAs.

Data Reduction

Questionnaires were checked for completeness and consistency. Very few errors were identified and these were mainly omissions of answers to particular questions in a very small (and statistically insignificant) number of cases. A detailed coding system was devised for the questionnaire and completed coding sheets were used for entering the coded results into the University of Manchester mainframe computer. Most questions had been designed to lend themselves to easy coding, although the desire to allow for multiple options on some questions (for example, reasons for being called names) meant that a substantial coding process resulted.

Separate variables were allocated for all answers, thus allowing the greatest possible flexibility in analysing questionnaire data. The twenty-six questions in the questionnaire resulted in a total of 119 variables.

Although open-ended questions were kept to a minimum, there were some areas where it was felt students should be given the opportunity to give answers which might not fall into the categories provided. A sample of fifty questionnaires was checked and additional coding categories were created to allow for the inclusion of such responses. Seven questions required this form of analysis:

- Question 3 (*self-description in terms of ethnicity*) allowed students to add communities which they felt they belonged to but were not included in the list. Answers to this part of the question were grouped into additional categories. Included in these was a category for students who indicated that they were from mixed ethnic backgrounds.
- Question 4 (*self-description in terms of religion*) allowed students to add a religious community not listed. Additional categories were created based on responses. Where students had added a religious community which was deemed by the coder to be identical to an option already provided (e.g. where 'Islam' was used rather than 'Muslim') this was coded as such. However, no other assumptions were made about self-defined religious identity. For example, students who wrote in 'Catholic' or 'Greek Orthodox' were not assumed to be identifying with the broader 'Christian' category.
- Question 5 (*self-description in terms of linguistic community*) allowed students to add languages not listed. For coding purposes, additional languages were grouped under 'European', 'South Asian', 'Far Eastern', 'Middle Eastern' and 'African'.
- Questions 11, 14, 21 and 23 allowed students to enter reasons for receiving and giving abuse (*name calling; bullying*) in addition to those suggested. Additional answers were grouped for coding under nine additional categories.

The final three questions were totally open-ended, inviting comment by students on their likes, dislikes and any other feelings about life at school. Responses to these questions provided data of a more qualitative type which was drawn on for individual school portrayals. However, in order to test for any general patterns of response, these questions were also coded according to a list of categories derived from an initial analysis of a proportion of the questionnaires (although the list was expanded during the coding process).

Initially, a simple frequency analysis of the questionnaire results was produced for each school. Additional analysis of data by gender and ethnicity, and tests for degrees of significance in emerging patterns, were conducted for a selection of questions; the results of this analysis can be found in Appendix 4 (p. 153). Interview summaries were completed for all interviews drawing on notes taken during interviews and supplemented by additional material and verbatim quotes from tape recordings. These summaries were then analysed according to the key themes of the study. Although some quantitative data was extracted from these summaries (e.g. the numbers of teachers reporting attending INSET courses on aspects of cultural diversity) the main purpose of this material was to go beyond statistical analysis in order to understand the experiences of those involved.

Summary

Drawing on the various kinds of data generated by the research instruments, a portrait of each school was produced in terms of its inter-ethnic relationships. Key areas, and the various perceptions of these, which contributed to the emerging picture of the quality of inter-ethnic relationships in the schools, may be illustrated in the form of a matrix:

Table 2.1   Organisation of enquiry in schools

	Views and Experiences of				
	Heads	Teachers	Students	Researchers	Others
Levels of intercultural knowledge/ understanding					
Impact of LEA/school policies					
Influence of curricular and extra-curricular activities					
Teachers' experience and training					
Degree of inter-ethnic mixing					
The state of inter-ethnic relationships					
Special provision					

We do not claim to have used the matrix mechanically in our study, but it helped us (and may help the reader) to keep in mind both the dimensions of inter-ethnic relationships and the variety of source of perception about them encountered in our study.

As has been clear from the outset of our discussion, the focus of our study was the quality of inter-ethnic relationships between students in the nine schools. However, before we go on to look at the patterns of such relationships we need to understand something of the school contexts in which these relationships had developed. How well did the schools know themselves — their students and their staffs? What, if any, relevant policy frameworks did they operate with, and how widely were these internally known and acknowledged? To what extent were school staffs equipped by knowledge, experience, training and disposition to contribute positively to good inter-ethnic relationships?

For any school, addressing questions such as these is a necessary condition for defining and positioning itself as a setting for inter-ethnic encounters. We were therefore interested in exploring aspects of institutional self-knowledge, relevant policy and the preparedness of staff, across the nine schools involved in this study. Those are the foci of the next chapter.

Chapter 3

Preparing the Inter-Ethnic Setting:
Demography, Policy and Training

The title of this chapter suggests the artificial assumption that a school starts with a clean sheet, awaiting the arrival of a multi-ethnic student intake, and is in a position so to fashion the internal environment as to make it as encouraging as possible for good inter-ethnic relationships. We acknowledge that artificiality. All the nine schools we studied were going concerns, and none of them was remotely in a position to start at square one. Furthermore, all of them were more or less limited in their freedom of action in all sorts of ways, as any schools by definition must be. Nevertheless, in distilling material from our research which may be help-ful to schools, we thought it useful to work with a framework which would see the school as: a) increasing its potential for promoting good relationships; b) effect-ively managing aspects of its continuing operation which are relevant to, or criterial for, good relationships; and c) developing strategies for dealing with and improving the inter-ethnic encounter among its students. We suggest that fundamental to that agenda are: how well the school knows its students; what its policy orientation is and how its policies are formulated; and how well-equipped its staff are in relevant ways. In this chapter, therefore, we use our research to try to illuminate three main areas:

- the demographic profile of schools' students and teaching staffs — and how schools might inform themselves, reflect and act in that context;
- principles and policies relating to equal opportunities in general and repu-diation of racism in particular; and
- teachers' professional development, and their intercultural knowledge and experience.

Demographic Profiles of Students and Staff

It was noteworthy that none of the schools in the research was in a position to provide us with a definitive picture of the make-up of the school roll by ethnic group. (In some of the schools there was detailed and useful, though limited, information available — in particular, on the number of first languages spoken). Generally, it was not that the schools did not want to know more about their students' ethnic profile — there were plentiful examples of interest shown; but there was also evidence of uncertainty about aims and methods of generating information on the ethnic make-up of the school. In Chapter 4 below we give one or two examples to highlight the wide differences between schools in this context, as well as variations of perception within them. Although most headteachers and others with whom we discussed the matter acknowledged the need for more information, at only two schools were we given hard data, and at only a minority of schools were plans being made for systematic ethnic profiling of student intakes. Only one school was already operating a recognisable system of ethnic monitoring of its own.

At one school (Pine) the LEA return on students of 'overseas origin' did provide us with some worthwhile information, though comparison with the questionnaire returns indicated that the data in the school's possession was not up-to-date. For example, the item which asked students to decribe their ethnic group(s) showed a considerably larger percentage of students describing themselves as Bangladeshi than on the LEA return used by the school. This probably reflected the fluidity of admissions patterns. At Birch School full ethnic profiling had just begun, and accurate figures relating to the current first-year intake were thus available. The management at Beech School were awaiting computer software from the school's new LEA which would provide a database for ethnic monitoring. At the time of the research, the school interpreted 'ethnicity' purely in terms of students' first languages — and (to be fair) acknowledged that this was inappropriate. At more than one school, when senior managers were asked for this sort of information, we encountered vagueness compounded by buck-passing: 'Ask the heads of year; they should have a pretty good idea' was a not wholly untypical response.

In fact, none of the schools in the south kept records of the ethnicity of students. There was some evidence that relationships were 'better' in the southern schools than in the northern (this is explored in the next chapter) — from which it might be inferred that knowledge of ethnic profiles is relatively unimportant. We do not take that view: the more a school knows about its students' ethnicities, the more it is likely to be taking inter-ethnic relationships seriously. We acknowledge that the subject of ethnic monitoring is sensitive and we recognise that nationally, within the framework of equal opportunities policies and initiatives, the situation with regard to ethnic monitoring is dynamic. However, schools should — indeed must — know their students; that is the first prerequisite for providing an appropriate educational, and, as far as possible, social, environment for all of them. The relative difficulty we experienced in some schools in getting an accurate picture of their ethnic profile was, in itself, our first significant research finding: none of the schools knew the detailed pattern of their student intakes well enough. That finding correlated well with evidence (discussed later in this chapter) that teachers felt that they did not know enough about their students' cultural backgrounds.

Despite the lack of accurate statistical information, we found many examples of practical measures taken by schools to acknowledge the presence of ethnic minorities; there were also many cases of failure to do so. Some schools responded positively to a large minority language presence — for example (at Elm School) by using Bengali widely alongside English in displays of students' work and providing a curriculum option in Bengali. On the other hand, there were schools which seemed not to be coming to terms with increasing proportions of ethnic minority students. For example, Pine School continued to issue a detailed handbook for students and parents which seemed to make no concessions to those with other than a high level of formal competence in English. Further examples of a positive and negative kind are discussed in later chapters.

Some schools took much trouble to communicate with parents across the communities — as illustrated by Ash School where there was an active PTA whose main emphasis appeared to be involvement of parents of all backgrounds in school life. During the research period a community evening took place which attracted about 200 parents, and included a Sikh band, a black teacher reading some of her poetry and a Rap singer who had been a student at the school. Another school (Birch) communicated very actively with parents in general, issuing regular reports, letters and a monthly newsletter, and running a range of social activities organised by a School Association. It had been trying in recent years to do something about its relative (and admitted) lack of success in developing relationships with the increasing number of Asian parents. Strategies adopted included co-option of ethnic minority representatives onto the governing body, and issuing newsletters in community languages. Although the school's success in involving parents from the minority communities was still limited, the level of determination appeared to be as high as in any of the schools studied, and higher than most. And it was by no means the only school reporting real difficulty in making contact with Asian parents. Some schools reported difficulties in developing relationships with ethnic minority parents whose own limited educational experiences proved a barrier to them feeling at ease in school. Other schools had attempted to draw on minority languages in translating letters and newsheets only to discover that many parents, particularly those from Bengali communities, were not literate in their mother tongue.

In general, it appeared that the more ethnically diverse a school was, the less sustained and proactive it seemed to be in its communication with ethnic minority parents as ethnic minority parents. This state of affairs could be explained by a lower sense of urgency about the matter in schools where the pattern of ethnicity was comparatively fragmented and varied compared with schools where there was a large and to some extent unitary constituency to consult. Another overlapping explanation might be that the highly diverse schools tended to be located in areas of longer-established multi-ethnic settlement, where minority communities were less self-contained. But neither of these explanations justifies the failure of a school to strive for effective communication with all of its parents and the communities they represent. To be fair, we encountered numerous particular examples of good communication with parents at the highly diverse schools — in many instances more successful than at the others.

Awareness of and sensitivity to religious diversity was apparent in some schools. In one case, the research period coincided with preparations for Ramadan. Students were gathered in the hall and the school's policy was explained to them, copies being distributed in English and Bengali. Staff were encouraged to respond sensitively to issues associated with fasting. In another (Church of England) school, admissions policy entailed deliberate reservation of a quota of places for students from backgrounds of other faiths, and the school's prospectus committed it to 'the promotion of a greater awareness of the multi-cultural, multi-religious nature of contemporary British society'. The school rules included the item: 'jewellery (except for religious items like Sikh bangle, cross and chain) should not be worn'. There was considerable variation between schools, and some inconsistency within them, as far as recognition of religious diversity was concerned: extra-curricular activities, for example, did not always take account of the special position of Muslim girls, even at schools where, for example, minority religions' festivals and observances were publicly recognised and even celebrated. In all the schools, however, religious dietary laws were respected.

We turn now to the ethnic profiles of teaching staff. We found extraordinary variety across the sample of schools: at Pine School, where over half of the students were from ethnic minority backgrounds (Bengali Muslims being the largest single group) there were no ethnic minority teachers in an establishment of eighty-five, and most of the staff had taught at the school since its days (long gone) as an all-white grammar school. At Beech School, which was rather similar to Pine in its student intake, there were an estimated seventeen ethnic minority teachers out of a staff of seventy — thirteen south Asian, two Afro-Caribbean, one Turkish and one Greek. At Elm School, which again had a large Bengali student intake, there were no established members of staff from Asian backgrounds, but two were of Afro-Caribbean origin. There were, however, a number of Section 11 Bengali-speaking language support staff — as there were at Beech School. However, there was an important difference between Elm and Beech: the Bengali language support teachers at Beech seemed to be highly marginalised. They were all women, and tended to be treated disrespectfully by the Bengali boys in classroom situations which we observed (boys were in a large majority over girls at Beech) and ignored by other students. On the whole they did not seem to be well-integrated as members of staff, and there were apparently no exceptions. At Elm, on the other hand, a Section 11 teacher of Bengali Muslim background was extensively involved in school life and her support was frequently mentioned by other teachers during interviews.

In Ash, Yew and Birch Schools where there were at most two established teachers of ethnic minority origin, and in the case of two schools no Section 11 or similar support staff in the schools. The difference between the ethnic profile of staff in these northern schools and those in the south was quite remarkable. Beech School has already been mentioned; in every other southern school there was a substantial proportion (roughly one-sixth to one-fifth) of teachers of ethnic minority origin. In three of the four southern schools a number of them were in quite senior positions (including heads of year and department, and an acting deputy head of school). At one of them the principal and senior laboratory technicians were of Afro-Caribbean and south Asian origin respectively.

That major difference between the ethnic profiles of staff in the northern and southern schools is difficult to explain. The fact that most of the southern schools were also more ethnically diverse in their student composition than their northern counterparts is not necessarily relevant. In any case, Beech, with its seventeen ethnic minority teachers and an absolute majority of Bangladeshi students, was a notable exception to that pattern. We suggest three interconnected factors that may have been relevant. First, all the southern schools were in greater London and benefited from the mobility and cosmopolitanism that this implied. Second, the southern schools had a much longer track record of comprehensivisation and multi-ethnic intakes than all except, perhaps, one of the northern schools. Third, the relatively high staff turnover in the south compared with the northern schools (the average age and length of service of staff in general in the south were considerably lower than in the north) meant that there must have been more opportunities for teachers from ethnic minority communities in the London schools.

Whatever the explanation of these differences (if there is one) it is essential to clarify what it is exactly that we advocate as far as recruitment of ethnic minority teachers is concerned, and why we think it is important for inter-ethnic relationships. Before embarking on this research, we might have accepted as axiomatic the proposition that a school with a significant proportion of ethnic minority students should seek to recruit significant numbers of ethnic minority teachers. (Indeed, we would have wanted to accept the wider proposition that, for the sake of education for cultural diversity in *all* schools, ethnic minority teacher recruitment should be a conscious feature of any school's staffing policies). Our experience of studying inter-ethnic relationships in these nine schools has not changed our general view but it has given us a sharper sense of what may be appropriate and inappropriate; productive and counter-productive. To start with, if ethnic minorities are under-represented on a school's staff, the school should do everything short of illegal reverse discrimination to redress that imbalance (by 'under-representation' we simply mean a lower level of representation than the proportion of ethnic minorities in the population as a whole). This is nothing more than a policy of promoting equal opportunity in a society whose ethnic minorities have been the disproportionate victims of inequality and it is to be justified in terms of that general principle. But there is also a specific justification — at once social and educational — for such a policy: that a school should *exemplify*, not just deliver, a multi-cultural education. That would be right for any school; it is self-evidently right, then, for a school which manifests ethnic diversity in its student intake. And those rather formal arguments leave out of account the fact that, under the right circumstances, the presence of ethnic minority teachers is good for both students and the staff as a whole.

Admittedly, the task of recruiting ethnic minority staff is a difficult one, and any discussion of the difficulties is beyond the scope of this study. But we feel confident that any school in a similar position to those we studied where there were a large number of ethnic minority students and hardly any such teachers, should examine its values and procedures very carefully, to ensure that everything is done within its power to attract, recruit, motivate and retain ethnic minority staff.

That prescription is easy both to preach and to accept. We do not minimise the difficulties involved in its implementation. But the research reinforced our view that a substantial presence of ethnic minority teachers in a school is both appropriate and productive if such teachers are *in every sense part of the establishment.*

Wherever we saw Afro-Caribbean or Asian or other teachers from minority back-grounds being fully involved in every aspect of school life (whether or not they were in relatively senior positions) we could see a healthy situation. Where we felt that ethnic minority staff were in a school to do a particular job only with minority students, on fixed-term contracts and not mixing socially in the staffroom and at school events — in short, marginalised — there we could see a situation which we believed to be unhealthy. Not only was it undesirable for the individuals concerned, it was bad for the school and its students, precisely because these staff were seen as marginal. That is not to say, for example, that there should have been no Section 11 support staff in a school; but everything depended on how a school was disposed and able to treat such staff (we use the past tenses here, simply because at the time of revising material for this book, we have become aware of the scaling-down of Section 11 support by government to local authorities).

In a number of professional contexts it has become common to see groups of workers examining their behaviour as groups, through focused activity, concentra-tion purely on the behaviour of the group itself without reference to a task, and development of awareness of group processes in ordinary task-related contexts such as meetings. Management courses — including those on educational management — often deal with aspects of individual/group behaviour in professional settings; but we do not believe that group self-examination is yet as much of a feature of institutional behaviour in mainstream school education as it is, for example, in therapeutic communities for disturbed young people, or in the social work profes-sion. The relationship between a school and its ethnic minority teachers is exactly the sort of focus on which analysis of group behaviour by the group — appropri-ately facilitated as necessary — should be able to throw light (there are, of course, many other aspects of staffroom and management behaviour and relationships which could similarly benefit). The point of this is to see what might be done to make inter-ethnic relationships among the staff of a school as good as they can be, so that the best possible example is set to the students. We should certainly have favoured some group self-analysis in one or two of the staffrooms of our research sample (those in which ethnic minority staff appeared most marginalised). Others, we are happy to say, were models of ubiquitous sociability.

Finally in this section on the ethnic profiles of schools and staffs, we must emphasise that our research schools differed markedly in the extent to which they were in a position to control their ethnic and other kinds of intake profile. For example, Beech School's freedom of action was very limited, compared with that of Yew School, with regard to the ethnicity, 'ability' and socio-economic mix of its student intakes. That sort of difference can be found all over the country. Government policy on the organisation of secondary education — especially the injection of 'market forces', the assault on LEAs and support for grant maintained schools in practising new forms of selective admission — is likely to exacerbate that Darwinistic tendency. Even if the likeliest candidate for good inter-ethnic relationships is a school with a thorough student mix of ethnicity, 'ability' and socio-economic backgrounds, together with a cosmopolitan staffroom, there is clearly no point in just calling on schools to acquire those characteristics. But it would seem reasonable to expect schools to know and understand as much as possible about their intakes and to do everything in their power to make themselves a welcoming environment to *all* students, and to attract and cherish teachers from ethnic minority backgrounds.

LEA and School Policies on Equal Opportunities and Multi-Cultural/Anti-Racist Education

We begin with a brief mention of LEA policies on equal opportunities and 'racial' incidents. Although some institutional practice in this context will have been fashioned by its relationship to LEA policy documents, guidelines and directives over the last fifteen to twenty years, at the time of writing, the influence of the LEAs is in what may turn out to be terminal decline. The following remark made to us by a teacher at Oak School is only too likely to be justified many times over in the future:

> Is knowledge of cultures relevant? If so, how do I get information or advice? I never see an adviser in school. What's the point of an advisory service that is so overworked and understaffed that it can only cope with emergencies?

It remains to be seen whether the commercialisation of inspectorial and advisory services will adequately replace accountability of schools to LEAs, and LEAs' accountability to their electorates.

The research schools were situated in a total of six LEAs. All these were committed, at least on paper, to equal opportunities and the promotion of intercultural understanding. However, the approaches to policy development and implementation across the LEAs varied: some were relatively recent, and reactive — the most obvious example being Pine School's LEA, which already had a brief policy statement on multi-cultural education but was now developing a new policy document which took account of racism. Others were long-established and comprehensive. One northern LEA (to which Ash and Yew Schools belonged) had a long-standing record of response to cultural diversity. Multi-cultural, anti-racist and equal opportunities policies and programmes had existed for many years. Concern about developing and implementing appropriate policies had been strengthened by a recent serious racist incident in a secondary school in the LEA. Schools were required to log and report racist incidents. Birch School's LEA had drawn together a group of teachers to draft a multi-cultural education policy several years ago. The policy required all schools to promote regular discussion, strengthen links with the communities, prepare a clearly-stated policy, support teachers, and evaluate teaching styles and materials.

Certain of the LEAs were substantially involved in policy renewal and were adopting a strongly consultative approach: Elm School's LEA had produced a multi-cultural education policy statement some years ago and had designed a major project to encourage policy into practice. At the time of the research, a new consultative document on multi-cultural and anti-racist education had been produced and responses were being sought from teaching and non-teaching staff, governors, parents and members of local communities before it was presented to the council for adoption as formal policy. Beech and Oak Schools' LEA (a new one, set up with the demise of the Inner London Education Authority) was in the process of reformulating equal opportunities policy in education, in the context of long experience of developing such policy initiatives in welfare services generally. The LEA in which Fir and Larch Schools were located represented one of the most ethnically diverse areas of the whole country, and its policies were under continuous review. Much of its policy material stemmed from the Authority's Race Equality Unit, supported by the LEA's Multi-cultural Curriculum Support Group. (The latter, which has had a long history, has recently been closed down as a result of enforced cuts in local authority expenditure.)

Virtually all teachers interviewed in the research schools were aware that their LEA had a policy on equal opportunities, anti-racism and multi-cultural education. Many, on the other hand, felt uncertain about what was in it. There were wide differences between and within schools in teachers' evaluation of the LEA policies. The majority thought that the policy statements in themselves were satisfactory or good (as far as they felt able to judge); a minority felt that they were vague and platitudinous. A very common criticism was that the policy statements contained no suggested strategies for implementation; another was that LEA support for implementation at school level was inadequate. Many teachers expressed the view in interviews that the LEA policy was just a 'paper policy'. Terms such as 'vague generalisations'; 'toothless and watered down' and 'facile and superficial' were fairly common, as was the following sentiment:

> The object of the exercise was to produce a good document and then to
> sit back . . . There's no monitoring, evaluation or in-service plan built in.

In general, those who did know something about their LEA's policy often polarised into whole-hearted support or severe criticism — the latter being the majority reaction. The position taken depended very much on the individual teacher's own perception of appropriate responses to cultural diversity. Few of the teachers interviewed had been involved in the development of LEA policy and any sense of ownership was low.

Those who expressed support for LEA policies did so either because the policies were perceived to be uncontentious or were said to be moving in the right direction. Critics fell into three main camps: those who felt policies went too far, those who felt they did not go far enough, and those who doubted the value of policies at all. These were, of course, perceptions of teachers. Analysis of documents produced by some LEAs indicated that policies on equal opportunities and anti-racism were being developed and circulated to schools. The issue, even for those LEAs is how such policies should be owned and implemented by their teachers.

In addition, evidence from staff suggested that LEA INSET courses failed to tackle multi-cultural issues. As far as teachers were concerned, LEAs often suffered from what the Swann Report (DES, 1985) described as a 'credibility gap' between actual LEA practices and national pronouncements about multi-cultural education. It is clearly difficult to assess how far each LEA had gone in seeking to implement its own policy. However, these findings certainly demonstrate that it is one thing for an LEA to have a written policy and quite another to ensure that the policy is known and owned by teachers.

We turn now to school policies on equal opportunities, multi-cultural education and repudiation of racism. In interviewing teachers, we were interested to know what in the way of policies existed, whether the teachers were aware of them, whether they knew them in detail and how they evaluated them.

It became apparent from a variety of sources (mainly interviews and school documentation) that the nine schools differed from each other in terms of policy development in six main ways: the stage of their policy development; the degree of formality of policy articulation; the focus and scope of their policies; the degree of awareness and ownership of their policies among the staff; the way policies were generated and formulated, and the perceived effectiveness of policies.

To give some indication of the different stages in policy development in which we found the schools: Elm School was moving from an established multi-cultural education policy to a officially articulated anti-racist policy as part of a rolling programme of policy development. At Pine, a voluntary working group had been developing a multi-cultural education policy for some time. Ash School had adopted the LEA's equal opportunities and anti-racist policies. Yew had no formal policy on multi-cultural or anti-racist education, although it had clear statements about equal opportunities and respecting minority cultures in its prospectus. Birch was in the process of developing an equal opportunities policy to replace a multi-cultural policy as part of an ongoing policy programme. At Beech School, the staff handbook included sections dealing with equal opportunities and multi-ethnic education. The school's anti-racist policy had, we were told, developed through consultation with local community groups, youth groups and feeder primary schools. At Fir School, an equal opportunities policy had been written in 1984 when the foundation schools amalgamated, but there was no separate multi-cultural or anti-racist policy. Oak School had an equal opportunities policy, and this was given considerable emphasis in its Development Plan. Individual faculties at Oak School also included equal opportunities commitments in their faculty policy statements.

Most teachers in all schools were aware of the current situation with regard to policies in their own school. Sometimes, there was uncertainty about the actual nature of the policy or its status. For example, according to its headteacher, Larch School had an equal opportunities policy which embraced special needs, gender and culture. He saw that part of the policy which concerned us was anti-racist more than multi-cultural. A deputy head who had played a key role in developing the policy explained that it was felt that it would be 'unwieldy to have separate policies on race, gender, disability, etc.'. Almost all teachers at this school were aware of the school policy, although one preferred to describe it as 'a code of practice' and another 'a statement of principles'. A senior teacher who had been involved in the production of the document described it as 'a code of practice on anti-discrimination'. The deputy head mentioned above differentiated a code of practice from a policy by saying that, whereas a code of practice set out principles governing the social life of the school, a policy issued directives about curriculum. He did not believe that internal curriculum directives were necessary. He went on to say that, because the focus of the code of practice was on equal opportunities and not curriculum responses, in relation to ethnicity it was seen as anti-racist rather than multi-cultural. We assume that the rationale here was that 'multi-cultural' refers to curriculum content, and 'anti-racist' to interpersonal, intergroup and institutional behaviour.

Occasionally, teachers in those schools at which it was clear to us that policies or codes of practice existed said that they thought that there was no formal policy. In one case, as we have seen, there clearly was no formal policy; at Yew School, commitment to values of mutual respect, tolerance of ways of life and beliefs other than one's own was given high priority in the school's public documentation, and its abhorrence of racist behaviour was deliberately placed within the general disciplinary and pastoral framework of the school. Sometimes, however, teachers who were new to a school had an inaccurate or hazy idea of what was the case. In one school (Pine) a head of year said that there was no formal policy and added that the school did not highlight such things and 'everyone is treated the same'.

Modes of policy formulation varied considerably between schools, as might have been expected. To give two initial and contrasting examples: Ash School had adopted the guidelines provided by the LEA. In Elm School, teachers expressed different views about who was responsible for policy production, although all reported that every teacher had been given opportunities to comment, many adding that this was an important process if it were to be owned by all teachers. The school was engaged on a major rolling programme of policy production and evaluation.

The most frequently mentioned approach to developing policies in the other schools was through a working group. In Larch School, the (new) head reported that the equal opportunities policy had been written by a working party, chaired by a deputy head. A staff training day had been part of the process. Other staff explained that a policy had existed earlier but had been revised by this process. Almost all teachers interviewed were able to comment on the policy, and there was a general feeling that all staff had been involved in the process. However, there was much variation in the assessment of the degree of involvement and the relative input from senior staff, the working group and other teachers. Most teachers described the role of staff in general as endorsement — after the policy had been written and before it was taken to the governing body. There was some concern expressed by support staff who felt that they had not been involved in the staff training day for the policy. The headteacher, senior staff and a member of the working group interviewed all felt that staff had a positive attitude to the policy and were supportive. Several teachers suggested that this was because of the personal commitment and calibre of teachers rather than the policy itself. One teacher was certain that there was little ownership of the policy and a black teacher doubted that the policy had changed the negative expectations which some teachers had of black boys.

At Pine School, most staff mentioned the working party on multi-cultural education. Several meetings of this group took place during the research period. It was a voluntary group mainly of 'enthusiasts' but was given more formal status by being chaired by the headteacher. Observation of meetings during the research period revealed a high degree of commitment on the part of those involved, but some tensions, particularly between advocates of liberal pluralist approaches emphasising curriculum content, and those favouring a tougher anti-racist position. There were also 'moderates' and 'radicals' on the question of monitoring the implementation of policy. The use of a working group to develop policy was seen as a weakness by some teachers. One commented, 'It was developed by a group of enthusiasts and therefore has not been owned by the staff.' The head of middle school said:

> The group is voluntary and there are no heads of department on it. The members are seen as enthusiasts and there is little general ownership. It needs a more powerful voice.

There was also a feeling among teachers that cultural and 'racial' matters were primarily the concern of Section 11 staff (something commented on with concern by a Section 11 teacher).

An equal opportunities policy was also being developed at Birch School through a working group. This was indeed part of a whole-school approach to policy development — working groups' decisions and recommendations being fed back to all teachers through faculties. The official school view was that the working group was an informal discussion group open to all members of staff. However, discussions with teachers revealed that often they felt that the group had more established legitimacy than the official view suggested. Several teachers felt that the primary concern of the equal opportunities group was with gender issues. While its voluntary nature inevitably meant that it tended to attract 'enthusiasts' rather than a full cross section of staff, the fact that one of the deputy heads chaired meetings and the headteacher was committed to it (and often attended meetings) meant that it was seen as more than a talking shop. Two meetings of the group were held after school during the research period. On both occasions an open invitation was posted on the staffroom noticeboard. Six teachers attended the first meeting which was mainly concerned with the Policy and Development Plan. The second meeting took the form of a discussion about the implications of equal opportunities for school uniform. About twenty teachers attended this meeting, which was lively and well-structured.

The brief descriptions above illustrate the strengths and weaknesses of working group approaches to bring about change. The voluntary nature of the groups meant that attendance was irregular and not representative. While more teachers might attend meetings dealing with specific practical issues (particularly if they were perceived to be 'problems'), they tended to miss out on the more philosophical and political debates about multi-cultural education, anti-racism or equal opportunities. In addition, once a working group gained an image of consisting of 'enthusiasts' or even teachers with a particular line on such issues, other teachers might easily become alienated. However, the strength of the working group approach, particularly when supported by senior management, lay in the opportunity it extended to a large number of teachers to participate in discussions about policy. Provided a school is aware of the potential disadvantages of the approach, and ensures that at appropriate intervals the group can 'speak' to all staff, working groups can play a good part in developing a wide sense of ownership of policy change and development.

A great deal depends, however, on *how* a working group performs its task. It is difficult to overrate the importance of understanding group behaviour in professional situations. We have already expressed the view that an equal opportunities (or any other) working group is unlikely to achieve very much without some real reflection on the dynamics of group behaviour and, if necessary, appropriate training. That reflection must take place *in the group*, though it may, of course, be accompanied by facilitation of an appropriate kind. This is particularly important in the context of an area such as equal opportunities policy. Members will bring to such a group a variety of ideological and personal basic assumptions, interests they want to defend, spectres they want to exorcise and emotional hand-luggage they do not want to part with. Whether and to what extent a group initially characterised only by the basic assumptions of each individual member can become a proper working group, will dictate its degree of success.

Assessment of the *effectiveness* of school policies varied across and within the nine schools. Many teachers felt unable to make judgments, sometimes because policies were relatively recent or were being modified, or because no formal method of monitoring and evaluation had been instigated. Many comments were based on intuition and the teachers' particular views about the value or otherwise of policies. Two schools where views were strongly expressed were Larch and Oak Schools. At Larch School, teachers felt that students were aware of the policy. In the words of one teacher:

> This is the first school I've taught in where the kids are aware of the consequences of making racist comments . . . It's something that's taken ever so seriously by the school. People know it's the worst thing they can do, to make a racist comment.

The policy (or, rather, code of practice) was reported to have been discussed with students in tutorials. As an example of its reported impact, name-calling in the fourth year was said by one deputy head to have been 'virtually stamped out'. Comparison with the questionnaire responses on name-calling is instructive here: although the questionnaire results suggested no significant difference in the degree of name-calling at Larch compared with all but two of the other schools, the percentage of students who reported being called names at Larch because of race or colour was the lowest of all schools. Another illustration of the impact of the code of practice was the fact that commitment to equal opportunities was looked for in staff appointment interviews.

Senior staff were confident that the policy was effective:

> As a result of these policies, the school is a better place for the students to be ... Equal opportunities isn't something we bolt on any more. It's intrinsic in what we do.

In Oak School there was no general complacency: despite a number of positive views there were many comments suggesting that the policy was not very effective, mainly because it was not 'vigorously enforced' or monitored. A head of department commented:

> I often wonder whether it's just a paper policy. I've never been asked to account for and evaluate what the department is doing.

However, others felt that the policy was effective, partly because of committed staff, and partly because of the degree (unique in the nine schools) to which the students had been and were continuing to be involved in its development and implementation. A striking example of that involvement was provided for us by a student who told us that the headteacher had written a letter to all parents on behalf of the School Council about the school's stand against racist behaviour; she had been helped in the wording of the letter by some of the student representatives on the Council.

Teachers were asked what *value* they felt policies had in promoting good inter-ethnic relationships in schools. Often their assessment was based on the specific policies of their own schools. Within schools, teachers were frequently divided between those who felt policies had a lot of value, those who felt they had none and a larger middle group who felt that policies had some limited value.

In Elm and Yew Schools (very different from each other in terms of students' perceptions of inter-ethnic relationships) most teachers were optimistic about the value of policies. Flexibility and ownership were often said to be important. Ensuring implementation was also stressed. One teacher observed:

> If it is there then it must be accessible. It should be developed as part of everyday school life, not drawn on after the fact; after a problem has happened.

Several staff in these schools added that policies needed good quality teachers committed to their implementation. Many staff also mentioned the difficulty of keeping informed about policy development when they were subjected to so much bureaucratisation.

In contrast to those at Elm and Yew Schools, most teachers interviewed at Pine School felt that policies had little value, though some added that this was because of vagueness in the school's particular policy statements; or because it was not properly monitored. One teacher observed: 'It's not much use at present because it has not been discussed in full and is not owned by everyone'. Others felt that policies in general were not discussed sufficiently nor related to professional development programmes.

The fact that some teachers were unaware of, or vague about, their school's policy on equal opportunities, multi-cultural education, or anti-racism, was a cause for concern. It was understandable that, at a time when much was being asked of teachers and when policy writing and development was probably at an all time high, not all teachers could be aware of the details of all policies. However, it might be assumed that teachers would know at least that such policies existed. Those schools adopting policy production in the form of short, clear statements of aims, objectives and methods of monitoring would appear to be in a strong position. It must also be noted that some lack of certainty stemmed from the dynamic process of policy modification in which some schools were engaged — and that was to be welcomed. In practice, teachers were much more aware of the existence and detailed contents of their school policies than those of the LEAs. We agree with the composite view presented to us by many teachers: that the keys to effective policies are ownership, implementation and monitoring. There was no consistency across the sample in these areas, although clearly some schools were taking them very seriously.

The discussion above illustrates the complex range of views held by the staff interviewed on the value of explicit policies to do with race and culture. It has been argued that the development of a multi-cultural or anti-racist policy is one of the keys to promoting a holistic school response to pluralism (e.g. Willey, 1984; DES, 1985; Lynch, 1987; Shaw, 1990). Lynch (*ibid.*) also argues that such statements need to be firmly linked with a 'delivery document' which includes a clear description of the means whereby the school seeks to implement and monitor its policy. Some schools had gone some way in doing this. However, if the evidence from the teacher interviews reflects the general range of views in the schools then there is still work to be done in convincing some staff of the value of such policy statements, especially those who fear such policies may be counter-productive. This is particularly important if management teams are to win support for policies and their ownership by staff. The dangers of senior management trying to impose such policies was illustrated by the reaction of some teachers in Burnage High School resulting in the 'polarisation' of staff positions (Macdonald, 1989).

Teachers' Professional Development and Inter-Cultural Knowledge

We first examine the initial education and training of the teachers whom we interviewed in the nine schools. The Swann Report (DES, 1985) rightly argued that all initial teacher training institutions should include opportunities for teachers to explore the issues of education in plural Britain; should enable them to begin to address the particular educational needs of ethnic minority students, and should equip them also to give practical recognition to cultural diversity in their teaching in any school.

In all the schools, the majority of teachers interviewed said that their initial training had done almost nothing to prepare them to teach in multi-ethnic schools. It should be mentioned that the majority of these teachers had received their training more than twenty years ago, when issues of race and culture were on the whole not seriously addressed in training institutions. However, interviews with more recently trained teachers provided very little evidence to suggest that initial teacher training (ITT) was responding to cultural diversity in any substantial or consistent way. Often there was little difference in perception of the value of their ITT programme in preparing teachers for multi-ethnic schools between those trained very recently and those trained in the 1970s. For example, in Larch School, only three of the twenty-two teachers interviewed said that their course had been very effective. These teachers had all been trained between 1976 and 1979. However, recently trained teachers were more likely than older colleagues to comment on having gained some insights into this area, particularly if they had chosen a college or university in a multi-ethnic area. In Fir School, for example, four of the five teachers who said that their courses had dealt reasonably or very well with multi-ethnic matters were trained after 1980.

Those who reported that they had received some preparation often spoke of very small or optional aspects of their courses. A teacher whose course had only included one session on multi-cultural education had, along with other students, organised extra voluntary sessions on topics to do with ethnic diversity and racism. In the same school a recently trained teacher said that his course had been relevant but 'not very inspiring'. Others were critical of the approach adopted in their initial training. One ethnic minority teacher said his course had contained 'a little — but it was mainly rubbish. Liberal bullshit. I felt patronised'. Another recently trained ethnic minority teacher commented that her tutor 'did not agree with things like multi-cultural education' and had insisted that it was a matter of 'teaching children'.

Although some ITT programmes had responded to pluralism, only rarely had such perspectives permeated the whole programme or influenced subject specialisms. Similarly, teachers who had studied a first degree followed by· a PGCE frequently mentioned that their degree courses failed to deal with the international or multi-ethnic dimensions of knowledge and understanding. For example, in Fir School a recently trained science teacher contrasted an 'adequate' equal opportunities input in his ITT general course with the failure of his science curriculum and methods course to tackle such issues at all. However, a music teacher at that school had valued studying world music as part of an ITT course, and a senior teacher in Birch School said that although he had not been helped by his initial training he had encountered international and multi-cultural dimensions in his study of mathematics in his degree course and later studies.

A very small number of teachers said that they had received substantial help from ITT courses. At Yew School, a teacher who had taken a PGCE course five years before said it had dealt with such issues 'reasonably well' and added that multi-cultural aspects of the course had helped, but anti-racist elements had been disappointing and 'race awareness training tended to be a waste of time'. A black teacher who had trained in the late 1980s said that issues to do with race and culture had a high profile at a city-centre polytechnic and had been a very important aspect of the course. Booklets on race and culture had been produced and given to students. In addition, he had felt 'welcome' as an ethnic minority member on the course. Other teachers who had received some help explained that it was because they had chosen an optional course dealing with some aspect of cultural diversity or equal opportunities. Teaching practice placements in multi-ethnic schools had provided other teachers with some initial experience of cultural diversity.

The evidence from this sample supports the conclusion of the Swann report that initial teacher training had on the whole failed to prepare teachers adequately for teaching in plural Britain. All current ITT programmes are required to demonstrate that they include a multi-cultural and equal opportunities dimension; it may thus be assumed (though we do not do so with particular confidence) that all recently trained teachers will have received some preparation for teaching in multi-ethnic schools.

The introduction by the government of largely school-based initial training raises the question of whether and how student (or apprentice) teachers will in the future gain knowledge, critical understanding and experience in the areas of equal opportunities, ethnic diversity and multi-cultural education. In theory, there should be no problem: trainees will still spend time at the training institution, where contextual issues can be explored; and there will be more time than hitherto to gain the practical experiences of the relevant kind, through the much-increased proportion of time spent in school. In practice, however, we wonder whether this will indeed be the outcome of the shift in balance of training from the institutions to the schools: the more the trainees are seen as 'extra pairs of hands' (as student nurses used to be before Project 2000 was introduced — how paradoxical it is that ITT is going in the opposite direction to training for just about every other caring profession!) the less they are likely to be practically encouraged to engage with big and important cross-curricular issues in their training schools. Much will depend on how good the training schools are allowed to become. Resources will have to be injected at a level which enables such schools both to be going concerns for their staff and all their students, and laboratories for the apprentices learning their trade. Will that happen? And how long will it take for schools to become so well-equipped with teachers who have themselves undergone the relevant kinds of study, reflection and practical experience, that they will be able to offer apprentices a real chance to gain knowledge and critical insight in controversial areas such as equal opportunities?

A further issue arises from the relatively limited *breadth* of school experience student teachers are likely to have if the new system becomes fully established: opportunities to undertake substantial practice in a *range* of schools will surely diminish — with obvious implications for the degree to which ITT will equip teachers to work in multi-ethnic schools. For teachers who received their initial training before inclusion of those foci became a requirement in training institutions, continuing further professional development should clearly be a priority. However, when teachers in the schools we studied were asked about the degree to which external or school-based in-service education and training (INSET) was responding to matters of ethnicity, a mixed picture emerged.

The proportion of teachers who had attended a course dealing specifically with multi-cultural or anti-racist education varied substantially between schools. In Fir School, nearly two-thirds of the teachers interviewed had attended a course of this kind at some stage in their career. The head of that school argued that the LEA provided a lot of INSET geared to multi-culturalism and anti-racism and his views were supported by several teachers who had attended such courses recently. Most teachers had valued what they had learnt from LEA courses (although one teacher who had been to meetings of the LEA anti-racist campaigning group described it as 'alienating'). Attendance at such courses by two teachers had led to their appointment to posts of responsibility, and insights and understanding gained by others were often shared at school or departmental level. At Oak School, however, only four out of twenty-five teachers interviewed, and in Birch three out of twenty, had attended courses of this kind. In other schools, the proportions ranged from half to a third of teachers. Those teachers who had attended such courses often found them helpful in building up their knowledge, challenging attitudes and responding practically in school.

In Elm School, where about half of the staff had been on courses of this kind, all but one teacher described them as helpful, particularly in developing self-awareness. It is interesting to correlate that response with students' responses to certain items on the questionnaire. Although this school did not 'score' well in comparison with most others on the items dealing with perceived quality of inter-ethnic relationships and name-calling, it scored significantly better than all but one other school on the question: 'How much do . . . your teachers do to help you understand about the different . . . backgrounds of students in school?' At Larch school, about a third of the teachers interviewed had attended courses of this kind. According to a deputy head, it had been school policy for 'some time' to encourage staff to go on racism awareness courses (although this was not reflected in the type of courses which teachers reported attending in the last three years). Although the main benefit to the school was seen in terms of the increased awareness and competence of the individual teachers involved, reports were often produced and distributed and ideas gained shared with other staff. However, a black teacher felt that more use might have been made of the experience gained by the black teachers in the school from a pastoral course for black teachers run at the school by LEA.

Other teachers were more critical of courses. One had attended an LEA 'anti-racist' course several years ago. He described it as a 'roadshow' and added 'I did not like the spirit of the meeting. It was designed to hinder rather than encourage debate.' Another felt that a course he had attended had been 'too didactic' to be helpful.

Teachers were also asked if courses they had attended which were not specifically on multi-cultural or anti-racist education ever addressed issues of ethnic diversity. In Fir, Larch and Oak Schools teachers reported that many courses they had attended, particularly in arts, humanities and social science subject-based courses took into account anti-racist or multi-cultural issues, in some cases to a large extent. The exception was science, where several teachers reported having to raise issues which organisers had failed to include. Courses which were not subject based, such as TVEI and management courses, rarely addressed these issues.

Most teachers in all the northern schools reported that few general courses responded to cultural diversity. There were some exceptions to this including a drama course organised by an adviser who was familiar with the needs of multi-ethnic schools; an RE course which considered world faiths, and a language course which explored community languages. In addition, one teacher felt that many of the courses he had attended recently included a broad equal opportunities dimension. However, these experiences were not typical and many times teachers commented that unless they raised issues in courses they were rarely addressed.

The comments above are based on perceptions of courses as reported by teachers. Investigation of LEA provision suggested that attempts were often being made to meet the needs of teachers in multi-ethnic schools. In one LEA an ambitious rolling programme, run in conjunction with a nearby university and a polytechnic, was providing in-depth training for teachers. Key members of staff from a small number of schools attended each course and support for follow up, resources and evaluation was also provided. Other LEAs had advisers or advisory teachers developing their LEA's responses to pluralism, often through the provision of resource centres and short courses. Many of these initiatives were new and it is inevitable that unless a school makes attendance at such courses a priority, it would take many years for most teachers to benefit from them.

The pattern for the schools and LEAs in the present study showed some increase in the number of teachers who had received relevant INSET, compared with the picture presented by the Swann Report (1985, *op. cit.*). However, that Report's expressed hope for the permeation of all INSET with multi-cultural sensitivity had yet to be realised for most teachers in this sample. Stone and Pumfrey (1990) suggest that the problem is even more widespread and that 'relatively few in-service training programmes include effective minority language and culture awareness courses.'

The pattern of INSET has changed radically in the period since this research began. Changes in the political and financial context in which schools work have entailed severe reductions in LEA INSET provision, and a shift to individual school- and consortium-based programmes. In interviews, teachers were asked to what extent INSET work organised by their schools took into account cultural diversity.

To deal first with courses *not* specifically on that theme: in more than half of the schools in the sample (Elm, Ash, Yew, Larch and Birch) most staff said that although few internally-organised INSET courses dealt specifically with multi-cultural or anti-racist education, all courses inevitably took on board the implications for teaching in a multi-ethnic school. In the words of one: 'Even if you don't start by looking at it, it always comes in!' In one school (Birch) which had not provided whole-school INSET on multi-cultural or anti-racist education, two-thirds of the teachers interviewed said that the issues were raised at faculty level. However, in terms of structured or planned responses, the amount of attention paid to such issues varied between departments in these schools. Teachers' perceptions of the same courses sometimes gave conflicting views about the degree to which matters were addressed. Often heads of departments gave a more generous assessment of their inclusion than other teachers. Variations were no doubt due in part to the degree of importance attached by teachers to such issues and their assessment of the value of discussions which arose incidentally and those which had been planned as an integral dimension of the courses.

In the other schools (Pine, Fir and Oak) although some general courses were described as taking account of cultural diversity, most were described as taking little or none at all. In Fir School concern was expressed by several teachers that courses tended to focus on management, administration and planning. In Pine, several teachers felt that school-based INSET did not respond well to issues of race and culture. Two teachers in particular were very critical, one commenting that the response to cultural pluralism was 'pragmatic', the school only dealing with issues if they happened to arise.

In most schools, INSET tended to be based on departmental needs and often related to curriculum subjects. However, whole-school themes were also addressed, and in some schools aspects of ethnicity and education were included. In three schools (Elm, Pine and Ash) courses dealing particularly with language awareness had been set up, in two cases by Section 11 teachers. Thus virtually all staff in these schools had recently experienced a course dealing with pluralism. Responses in all three school were generally very positive, particularly about the way the courses had helped teachers' self-awareness. Again, it is worth drawing attention to the fact that, at Elm and Pine Schools, students were significantly more positive than in all the other schools on the questionnaire item dealing with the extent to which teachers helped with inter-cultural understanding.

Other schools provided less in the way of specific courses. At Oak School only two teachers said they had attended a school-based INSET course on multi-cultural or anti-racist education. At Pine, a survey of felt needs had placed multi-cultural education in the top three areas. A working party had been set up, but specific INSET work had been difficult to arrange because of more pressing demands. At Yew School, several teachers mentioned that issues to do with race had been raised but so far no courses had been set up. In Birch, where none of the teachers interviewed reported attending in-school courses on such topics, several teachers explained that it was less a problem of commitment and more a problem of time:

> Multi-cultural education is a priority but it is halfway down the list. We are under pressure to get through the basics so it would be a luxury.

School-based courses often dealt with the broad issues of equal opportunities. This was seen by teachers as having both advantages and disadvantages. Teachers often argued that dealing with matters of ethnicity under the wider umbrella was seen as less threatening and tended to involve more staff. At Larch School a staff training day on 'dealing with discrimination' was described by a deputy head as 'the best INSET day the school has had'. Issues which arose then continued to be addressed by the equal opportunities working party. Many other teachers in the school mentioned this particular course, although perceptions of its emphasis and value varied. Several teachers commented that the course focused on gender issues rather than those associated with race and culture, some observing that it reflected the way in which they felt gender issues dominated school debates on equal opportunities. One teacher commented:

> Anti-racism is fairly marginal to INSET courses . . . We spend far more time discussing sexism whenever we discuss equal opportunities because we have a lot of women in teaching and we don't have a lot of black teachers. There are far more people who feel confident and competent to discuss sexism . . . so we end up with a one-sided approach.

In another school, an ethnic minority teacher felt that the developing emphasis on equal opportunities was deflecting concern from important work in multi-cultural and anti-racist education because the issues were so wide and tended to be dominated by gender. In Fir School, where most staff interviewed said that they had not been on any in-house INSET dealing explicitly with multi-cultural education, gender issues had been a recent focus of equal opportunities INSET work. A half-day course had been run and followed up by a working group. For many of the teachers in this school, equal opportunities had not been associated with race and culture. In Yew School, almost all the teachers interviewed mentioned a course on equal opportunities, many commenting that the focus had been mainly on gender.

The *relevance* of teachers' initial training and further professional development to inter-ethnic relationships in a school is not self-evident. We are certainly not in a position to argue a tight correlation between amounts of appropriate ITT and INSET experienced by teachers and quality of inter-ethnic relationships among students. Differences in perceived quality of relationships between the schools, on the evidence presented so far, were much greater than differences between the schools in patterns of relevant ITT and INSET. But it can be argued that the level of a teacher's knowledge and understanding of students' ethnic and cultural backgrounds is relevant to the quality of inter-ethnic relationships: teachers have to deal with a wide range of situations in which that knowledge and understanding must help; they also set examples, and the more they are in a position to exemplify inter-cultural understanding, the more influence they will be able to bring to bear on the complexion of relationships in their schools. We therefore sought to gain a picture of the level of knowledge teachers felt they had of the ethnic and cultural backgrounds of their students. (We shall be dealing with *students'* inter-cultural knowledge and understanding in Chapter 5, as we examine curricular and other related aspects of the school's operation as an inter-ethnic environment).

Correlated with the fact that students tended to see planned provision by the school as a limited source of knowledge and understanding of others' cultures (see Chapter 5) were teachers' own confessions of ignorance in this area. There were varied amounts of information available to teachers (for example through multi-lingual information and resources, material on religions, resources supplied by local communities reflecting students' cultures, relevant publications in staffroom and library, etc.). That variation is to be seen against the relative dearth of professional development courses in aspects of ethnic diversity and their educational implications, across all of the schools. Interviews with teachers revealed that, while many of them were knowledgeable, experienced and sensitive in one relevant way or another, this was due much more to long experience of working in inner-city multi-ethnic and multi-faith situations, or to other relevant life experience, than to specific and substantial professional development in which learning more about students' cultural backgrounds was a major element. Overall, then, teachers tended to express a lack of sufficient knowledge of their students' cultural backgrounds. It is therefore not surprising that (as we shall see) on the whole students tended to see their own inter-cultural knowledge as arising more from life than from planned school provision.

We accept that the relationship between knowledge on the one hand and attitudes and behaviour on the other is not an easy one to posit. Our research bears that out. We shall see, for example, in Chapter 5 that differences between schools in apparent quality of relationships did not correlate in any obvious way with the different amounts of multi-cultural education going on in the schools. Nor could we say with confidence that the undoubted limitations in teachers' inter-cultural knowledge were holding the schools back in terms of their inter-ethnic relationships. But we found enough examples of dedicated and highly knowledgeable teachers, full of insight into their students' varied backgrounds and needs, to convince us that if teaching staff in general are enabled to rise to the level of the best in that respect, the impact on relationships might be considerable — even, perhaps, spectacular.

In this chapter we have been concerned with some of the ways in which a school 'prepares' itself as a setting for inter-ethnic encounters, by means of: knowing its intake; recruiting its staff; formulating and disseminating its policies; and sharing with its teachers responsibility for their professional development and their growth in knowledge of students' cultures. In all these areas there was clearly room for improvement in all of the schools. They did not know enough about their intakes; they either had few ethnic minority teachers, or revealed shortcomings in the way they treated them; they were not always effective in their policy formulation and implementation; and too many of their teachers were insufficiently prepared to work with maximum effectiveness in the multi-ethnic setting. None of the schools, then, was yet a wholly suitable and welcoming environment for multi-ethnic education and inter-ethnic relationships.

That is, of course, a bald catalogue of criticism. It must be balanced by acknowledging the evidence of good work being done in all these areas — as the examples given in the chapter illustrate. But the point of the criticisms is, of course, to highlight what we believe are some of the priorities for any school with a significant proportion of students of ethnic minority origin, which seeks to be as far as possible the right sort of environment.

We have yet to set out a range of further factors which we believe to be relevant to good inter-ethnic relationships, and on which we were able to gather suggestive data from our study of nine schools. That will be the main business of Chapters 5 and 6. It is, however, perhaps timely to pause, and place before the reader now the many-sided picture which emerged of the quality of those relationships, as perceived by teachers, students and ourselves; and to do some preliminary analysis of the patterns of similarity and difference within and between schools in the perceived quality of inter-ethnic relationships. Those will be the tasks of Chapter 4.

Inter-Ethnic Relationships in the Schools: Perceptions of Quality

The picture that will emerge in this chapter is complex and at times contradictory. We are cautious about making even tentative generalisations about, for example, the quality of relationships in one school or in all of them, or about teachers' views as compared with students', or about regional differences. That reflects not only the great variety of *perception* of the quality of relationships within as well as between schools, but also the various messages which arose from the different methods of enquiry adopted. In the use of the quantitative data, based on analysis of questionnaires with a large sample of students (c.2300), we have tried to avoid 'sacrificing understanding on the altar of description' (Troyna, 1991: see our methodological discussion in Chapter 2). Thus, on the one hand it may safely be said on the basis of questionnaire responses, interviews and group discussions that most students and most teachers in all of the schools felt that the quality of inter-ethnic relationships was quite good. On the other hand, this very general picture masked wide differences of opinion, and sometimes wide conceptual differences, between and within schools, and between and within student and teacher groups. The questionnaire data proved useful in eliciting from a large sample a broad pattern of student response on a number of key issues, and some patterns of significant difference between schools and between different ethnic groups. Interviews and discussions with students and teachers revealed more of the texture of those differences than could have been expected from the quantitative data. However, that data was valuable in providing a background of suggestive patterning.

The questionnaire administered to all year 8 and year 10 students asked them to say (on a four-point scale) how well they thought students from different backgrounds or religions got on with each other (Appendix 3: student questionnaire, Question 9). The results were quite striking: 58.9 per cent of all students chose the 'quite well' option; another 28.5 per cent said that students got on 'very well', and only 11.1 per cent of all students said that they got on 'not well' or 'not at all'. This sort of statistic matches rather well the findings on the incidence of 'racism' in secondary schools reported in the studies by Kelly (1990) and Smith and Tomlinson (1989), and for the same reason should put us on our guard. Both studies reported that overt racism was not on the whole a large-scale problem in multi-ethnic schools. In our discussion of methodology in Chapter 2 we drew attention to Troyna's (1991) critique of assemblies of 'statistical data on the observable, detectable and easily measurable forms of racism'. Thus, just as it is unwise to infer from a relative scarcity of 'racist incidents' a low level of racism, it is equally unwise to posit good inter-ethnic relationships on the basis of a high level of reported general satisfaction. In this study, the amount of quantitative analysis conducted gave us our insight into the complexities of understanding inter-ethnic relationships, and challenged the simple picture presented by the response of the 'we get on quite well' sort. Interviews and discussions underscored that complexity, but also enriched the picture.

Table 4.1
Q.9: How well do students from different backgrounds or religions get on with each other?

	Beech %	Fir %	Larch %	Oak %	Elm %	Pine %	Ash %	Yew %	Birch %	All %
Very well	11.5	36.5	36	30.9	12.9	19.7	34	45.1	18.5	28.5
Quite well	52.1	57.4	58.1	60.7	64.7	66.2	54.6	51.4	66.8	58.9
Not well	27.1	3.7	4.8	6.2	17.2	8.3	6.9	1.9	10.7	8.8
Not at all	3.1	1.2	0.3	1.7	4.3	3.9	3.4	0.9	2.7	2.3

Table 4.1 shows the range of student questionnaire responses on how well students from different backgrounds got on with each other, for each of the nine schools, and for all schools combined. We shall use that as a starting point for further analysis, focusing initially on inter-school differences.

Are there any *significant* differences between schools in that table? This question will be taken up a little later. There certainly are some *striking* differences: of the southern schools (Beech, Fir, Larch and Oak) Beech clearly scores lowest on student perception of the quality of relationships, and the rest pretty high. Of the northern schools, Yew suggests a remarkably high proportion of students from different backgrounds getting on very well (the highest of all the nine schools); while Elm reveals a rather large number not getting on well. Among the nine schools, it is striking to observe that the two lowest scores on the 'they get on quite well' option (Yew and Beech) arose for opposite reasons: in the case of Beech it was because so many students felt that relationships were not good; in the case of Yew, because so many felt that they were *very* good. At the moment, we shall concentrate just on those two schools. *Why* were relationships, as reported by students, apparently so good in Yew School and so much less so in Beech School? How did interviews and discussions with students and teachers in those schools develop our understanding of the quality of relationships in them?

Beech School, which came off 'worst' in this item of the questionnaire, was largely 'bi-ethnic', with an absolute majority of Bengali students (50 + per cent), small numbers from other backgrounds and a large minority of white students. The overwhelming majority of students came from families in below-average to very poor economic circumstances. The spread of ability in student intake was not comprehensive, the majority of them being classified as 'band two and band three'. There was an annual student mobility rate of about 20 per cent. The local community was hardly a community; it was an inner-city area largely consisting of poor whites on the one hand and Bengalis from Bangladesh with a recent and current settlement profile on the other. The school's catchment area was thus not one of a long-established and settled multi-ethnic character. Communal tension outside the school was considerable. Difficulties between Bengali and white students (with Afro-Caribbeans and Turkish boys tending to side with whites) were noticeable and had spilled over into episodes of fighting not long before the research period. The amount of inter-ethnic abuse in the school seemed to vary in direct proportion to fluctuations in communal relationships outside.

The school was undergoing major changes, both external (change of LEA) and internal (changes in the senior management team) at the time of the research. In two key curriculum areas — music and home economics — there were unfilled vacancies for heads of department. Most of the senior managers, and two heads of department, were in 'acting' positions. There was no librarian, and the library was closed for most of the research period.

It is fair to say that Beech was trying to come to terms with its circumstances, both generally and in relation to its inter-ethnic situation. There were substantial references to anti-racism and equal opportunities in the staff handbook, and there was also evidence of support for victims of 'racial' incidents, as well as constructive (not just punitive) treatment of their perpetrators. However, although there were published policies and procedures for dealing with 'racial' incidents, it appeared that the school was not yet reflecting systematically on its ethnic make-up or on its inter-ethnic relationships: at the time of the research, the plurality of the school was measured purely in terms of first languages spoken (though it was the intention to change that). The abiding impression gained by the researchers was of an ethnically somewhat polarised school, in a transitional state, living (for the time being) uneasily with itself. Yet, despite all that, more than half of the year 8 and year 10 students (according to the questionnaire) felt that inter-ethnic relationships in the school were quite good.

Yew School, the 'best' according to the same questionnaire response, had a very different profile from Beech School, on objective criteria alone. In comparison with Beech, it was ethnically highly diverse. It was a young school, with a conscious (Christian) ethos which had developed out of inter-faith as well as ecumenical dialogue. Although a Church of England school, it was committed to drawing students from a wide range of ethnic and religious backgrounds. Students came from a much wider catchment area than Beech's, and therefore one which was inevitably less polarised in terms of ethnicity and more varied in economic profile. Its students came from as many as eighty feeder primary schools. Selection procedures (and the school was in a position to select according to chosen criteria) were formulated to achieve and maintain a wide ethnic and socio-economic mix, and there was a full spread of ability. Acceptance of non-Christian faiths, celebration of ethnic diversity and promotion of awareness of the multi-cultural nature of British society were given strong and public emphasis (for example, in the school's foundation charter). Attendance at parents' evenings tended to be high.

Although relationships at Yew School were perceived by students to be good or very good, there was no formal set of procedures for managing breakdowns in inter-ethnic harmony, except that guidelines to staff on disciplinary matters included a direction that all alleged racist incidents should be reported in writing to a deputy head. There was, on the other hand, explicit commitment to the application of democratic principles in the life of the school. The staffing was comparatively stable. In particular, the headteacher was strongly and publicly committed to equal opportunities and the celebration of ethnic diversity; and much of the moral tone of the school flowed from the strong leadership of the head.

Did the questionnaire results (just on that question) from these two schools really present a reliable picture of difference in quality of inter-ethnic relationships? Interviews with students and teachers indicate, not surprisingly, a more complex 'reality' than was presented by the statistical data, but on the whole tend to confirm its broad thrust. In Beech School, half of the teachers interviewed (fifteen out of thirty) described inter-ethnic relationships as less than satisfactory or poor. Furthermore, we felt that staff, and students, tended to interpret 'good relationships' negatively (no overt conflict; containment) rather than positively (mutual respect; collaboration; friendships and social mixing).

The headteacher at Beech (who retired during the period of research) spoke of community tensions reflected in the school as 'our West Side Story scenarios':

It's usually the whites against the Bangladeshis and the whites include Afro-Caribbean and Turkish . . . and that's how they perceive themselves in terms of gangs.

She explicitly dissociated the consequences of recent migration from racial prejudice and racist behaviour:

To the children it's not a question of race, it's a question of the latest group to come in and it's a question of territory.

In our view that statement, important though it was in exemplifying the negative experience of newer migrants to Britain, also (significantly, we believe) begged the question of whether those who experienced hostility and attacks in such contexts could be seen as anything other than victims of racist behaviour.

A teacher from the same school who described relationships as generally 'good' went on to say that things only looked good on the surface:

There's a sense in which on a day-to-day basis it looks OK, but there are deep-rooted prejudices especially among the white kids, so that when any particular difficulty arises they resort to open racism . . . in any moments of tension, then it all goes back to square one . . . and there have been some extremely serious confrontations and the rapidity with which things occur and increase in size so that it suddenly becomes an enormous problem and a huge confrontation on the streets outside, shows that there are very real problems.

We interviewed teachers who expressed negative views about the numerical dominance of Bangladeshi boys in the school. Other teachers expressed strong commitment to providing the best possible educational experience for the very many socially and economically disadvantaged students in the school. Some of those teachers also expressed frustration at the extent to which they saw that commitment thwarted by the school's short-term organisational difficulties, government legislation, lack of a unified equal opportunities ethos in the school and local tensions and conflicts outside the school.

Under half of the thirty-one students interviewed at Beech School described inter-ethnic relationships as 'good'. Fighting between Bangladeshi and white English students was the reason most often given by those who described relationships as 'poor':

They always fight about their religion and their colour.

Bengalis and English can't play together without fighting.

Some races are good to each other. Some — I mean the whites and the Bangladeshis — are born to be enemies.

The Bengali people hate the white people and the white people hate the Bengali people.

They don't like each other. Whites and blacks get on, but whites and browns don't.

During the period of research in the school we encountered a good deal of evidence — some of it at first hand — that older Bangladeshi boys were willing to defend their interests aggressively as a conscious reaction to their feeling of victimisation by whites; and that they were feeling their numerical dominance in the school as a source of strength. There could be little doubt that it was a reinforcer of negative feelings towards them by white and other students, some of whom said in interviews and discussions that teachers discriminated in favour of Bangladeshis. Whether it was true or not (and we did not on the whole feel that there was any partiality towards the Bangladeshi students), it was an uncomfortable reminder of what was thought to be one of the underlying causes of the Burnage tragedy (Macdonald, 1989) — a feeling on the part of the white community that their interests were ignored.

Notwithstanding the considerable difficulties faced by Beech School, there appeared to be much that it could build on, if allowed to settle down. The crucial requirements seemed to be: more stable staffing; a settled senior management team; a larger conception by the school of what it meant to be multi-ethnic and multi-faith, together with sensitive and informative systems of ethnic monitoring; the development of systematic policies and positive programmes for the encouragement of inter-cultural understanding and better relationships, and as much involvement with, and by, the local communities as possible. Although we encountered some negative attitudes towards ethnic diversity among staff, there was on the other hand no shortage of inter-ethnic goodwill among both staff and students.

At Yew School, over half of the teachers interviewed (nine out of fourteen) said that inter-ethnic relationships among students were good or very good. A deputy head linked this with the general philosophy of the school, saying with emphasis 'it's not an accident!' When asked for examples to illustrate good relationships, teachers frequently pointed to the high incidence of inter-ethnic mixing. A senior member of staff referred to sports teams, in which he said the degree of integration was 'terrific'. Another mentioned high attendance rates by ethnic minority students. He added that the Christian dimension was also important:

> The school is prayed for by families and churches. It adds texture; it keeps
> it from being a soulless place.

Overall, we got the impression that those teachers who felt positively about relationships in Yew School saw 'good relationships' as meaning more than just the absence of abuse or conflict. But some teachers did explicitly mention the lack of inter-ethnic 'unpleasantness'.

Discussions with staff about community links illustrated the fact that Yew was much less of a neighbourhood school than Beech: children were drawn from all over the town. Parents and families were seen to be the key links, rather than communities. Much effort seemed to be devoted to cultivating those links, and to (in the words of one of the deputy heads) 'learning how to get closer to what (the school) ought to be'. That propensity for reflection was well illustrated by the school chaplain's caveat about the need for realism about what the school could achieve:

> Schools ask too much of themselves if they think they can overcome the
> enormous pressure on families. School creates an alternative community.
> Students live their lives in two different communities. For many the school
> is a haven.

Another teacher said that students were likely to have better experiences in school than outside and that, for many, the school was 'an oasis of calm'.

Even in this school, which scored so highly in the student questionnaire, interviews and discussions with teachers revealed considerable variety of perception. Among those who felt unable to generalise about the quality of relationships, there were some who felt that groups of older black boys were insufficiently integrated into the life of the school and were not helped as much as they could be. A deputy head talked about them as a 'very vocal group' who were sometimes 'seen as threatening by other students'. Other teachers expressed the view that there was much room for improvement in terms of some of the *constituents* of inter-ethnic relationships, or major factors likely to affect the development of such relationships. Low levels of inter-cultural knowledge and understanding, and of ethnic minority representation among the staff, were two issues given some emphasis by teachers.

These issues arise at other points in this book, but staffing deserves a brief mention here. One senior teacher at Yew School reported that:

There are no Section 11 teachers. It doesn't fit in with the image the school wants to present of itself. And there's only limited E2L provision.

The contrast here with the substantial and highly committed E2L staff group at Beech School was arresting — even allowing for the considerably larger proportion of students at Beech who had little or moderate English proficiency. Furthermore, Yew School had only one ethnic minority teacher out of seventy, compared with seventeen out of seventy at Beech School. However, the majority of those seventeen at Beech were south Asian language support staff appointed to temporary contracts on a Section 11 grant. These teachers appeared to be marginalised both in classroom and staffroom (to a greater extent than the *established* group of E2L staff).

What of the thirty students who were interviewed at Yew School? Strikingly, all of them said that inter-ethnic relationships were 'good' or 'very good'. Many of them argued that they got on well because there were so many different groups in the school. The contrast of perception between these students and those interviewed at Beech School was instructive: among the latter, responses tended to focus on the encounter between whites and Bangladeshis; at Yew, students often commented on the way in which students from different backgrounds all mixed together. And reference to the multi-ethnicity of the school was typical:

> We get on OK. I don't know why. Possibly it's because there are loads of different races in school. We don't bother about skin, just personality.

Some edgy encounters between whites and Afro-Caribbeans were indeed mentioned by a few students. One or two referred to a 'black gang which goes after people — not just whites, anyone.' But that kind of interface between specific groups was given far less emphasis in interviews with Yew School students than at Beech. However, it should be remembered that at Beech School Afro-Caribbean students were seen as tending to align themselves with whites against Bengalis.

Many students commented on the impact of Yew School's overt ethos of equal respect for all:

> There are a few racists in school but they don't show their racism except maybe in name-calling. They know the school won't allow it.

> You're not allowed to be racist. You get the feeling that the school won't tolerate it.

> They tell you if you are racist what happens to you. They tell you in assemblies and lessons. The school makes a big thing about it if an incident happens.

Perhaps inevitably, the school's conspicuous value-position elicited a response in just one or two students that there was a tendency on the part of teachers to be harder on white than on black students.

On the central question of the quality of inter-ethnic relationships, the quantitative evidence, factual data about the two schools and material from interviews and discussions were on the whole well-aligned. Two preliminary (and not startling) conclusions from the analysis so far would seem appropriate here. Firstly, it may be significant that Beech was a largely 'bi-ethnic' school, in which ethnic polarity seemed to entail polarisation; while Yew was more truly multi-ethnic. Secondly, Beech was in a much weaker position than Yew to choose, in respect of so many of the elements that go to make up a school's effectiveness and even happiness. We hope that we have brought out enough in the way of differences in context, and differences of perception within, as well as between, Yew and Beech Schools to dismiss any suggestion about putting Yew at the top, and Beech at the bottom, of a 'race relations' league table. In concentrating so far on the direct question: 'how good are inter-ethnic relationships?', in just two of the nine schools, we have fulfilled our intention to start with something comparatively simple. We must now look at other dimensions of the analysis across the nine schools.

Table 4.2: Inter-school patterns
Q.9: How well do students from different backgrounds or religions get on with each other?

School	Elm	Pine	Ash	Yew	Birch	Beech	Fir	Larch	Oak
Elm		s−	h−	h−	/	s+	h−	h−	h−
Pine	s+		h−	h−	/	h+	h−	h−	/
Ash	h+	h+		h−	h*	h+	/	/	/
Yew	h+	h+	h+		h+	h+	/	/	h+
Birch	/	/	h*	h−		h+	h−	h−	/
Beech	s−	h−	h−	h−	h−		h−	h−	h−
Fir	h+	h+	/	/	h+	h+		/	/
Larch	h+	h+	/	/	h+	h+	/		/
Oak	h+	/	/	h−	/	h+	/	/	

Key to symbols:
s+ = significantly more positive than one or more of the other schools
h+ = very significantly more positive than one or more of the other schools
/ = no significant difference compared with one or more of the other schools
s− = significantly more negative than one or more of the other schools
h− = very significantly more negative than one or more of the other schools
* = pattern too complex to indicate overall positive or negative picture.

We turn next to comparisons between each school and all the others. We wanted to take advantage of the opportunity to see whether, on the basis of questionnaire data, there were statistically significant differences between schools, and between groups, in students' perception of the quality of relationships. That would, of course, stimulate further enquiry. Chi-square significance tests were carried out for each school against each other school for a number of the questionnaire items. The tests showed a higher frequency of significant or highly significant differences between schools than might have been expected. We shall focus for the moment only on Question 9. Table 4.2 shows the pattern of results for each of the schools in the left-hand column compared with all others (shown across the top row). Thus, for example, the table indicates that Yew School students' responses were very significantly more positive than those of Elm, Pine, Ash, Birch, Beech and Oak Schools. Conversely, Beech's students were very significantly more negative about relationships in their school than students in all of the other schools except Elm. Those patterns of significance link strikingly with the correlations in the earlier discussion between the quantitative and qualitative material from those two schools.

There are other patterns of significant difference, or lack of it, in Table 4.2 which are worthy of mention. One might have expected there to be significant differences between students' responses according to *region*. But the significance for the northern schools against the southern schools, and vice-versa, was negligible: looking at all nine schools in this piece of analysis, we found that the northern schools came out slightly 'worse' than the southern schools for students' reported view of the quality of inter-ethnic relationships, but not to an extent remotely near statistical significance.

A different statistical picture emerges, however, if Beech and Yew Schools, which (as we have already seen) were at opposite ends of the spectrum and which bucked any possible regional trend, are excluded. The three remaining southern schools 'score' significantly 'better' than the four remaining northern schools. It might be tempting, but would be quite wrong, to say that that was because, in general, they do things better in the south — wrong both *a priori* and because that was not our experience. It would be premature to say too much at this stage about what it is about a school which makes its students feel that they get on well — except that we believe that the explanation of those statistically significant differences between schools, as demonstrated in Table 4.2, must lie partly in schools' demographic intake profiles and the socio-economic characteristics of their catchment areas (both of those factors are wholly unsurprising: the former is explored elsewhere in this book, and, whilst we acknowledge the latter, it was not a main focus of this study).

The responses from students who were interviewed compared well on the whole with the evidence from those significance tests: we could discern no particular regional tendency in their expressed views. Interviews with teachers, on the other hand, *did* suggest a regional pattern: in four of the five northern schools — Elm, Pine, Ash and Birch — most teachers reported that inter-ethnic relationships were neither particularly bad nor particularly good. In three of the four southern schools — Fir, Larch and Oak — most of the teachers interviewed described relationships as good.

There were, of course, many exceptions to that pattern: the most obvious were Beech and Yew Schools, where *all* the evidence we collected suggested that each of those schools was to some extent *sui generis*. In Elm and Birch Schools (north), several teachers gave specific examples of 'genuine' or 'deep' friendships which had developed between students of different ethnicities. Conversely, some teachers in Larch and Oak Schools (south) expressed serious reservations about student-student relationships: at Larch, several teachers talked about the abuse directed at African students by Afro-Caribbeans:

> The size of their lips, noses, their blackness — they do it to each other as well. The worst thing a West Indian boy can call another is a Black African. When you are doing the register and when you get to X (African name) and other African names there's a general sort of tittering and sniggering.

Other teachers in the same school mentioned mutual abuse between members of those two groups, and between 'Africans and Indians' and 'Muslim and Christian Cypriots'. And a teacher in a southern school (Oak), where twenty-three of the twenty-five teachers interviewed described relationships as satisfactory to very good, emphasised students' lack of tolerance of each other's beliefs and referred to *intra*-group solidarity and *inter*-group hostility in the school — illustrating well the variation of perception within schools. A further illustration was provided by two teachers in Elm School, where most teachers interviewed reported satisfactory relationships on the 'negative' model at best (absence of conflict rather than positive interaction). One of the two teachers spoke about 'an undercurrent of mutual tolerance', and the other 'an undercurrent of mutual harmony', among students.

So, despite a certain amount of evidence suggesting *some* regional difference in perceived quality of inter-ethnic relationships, the evidence was inconclusive. As we shall see a little later, apparent regional differences were more likely to reflect other features of the sample of schools used in the research.

If regional differences were not in themselves significant, did the variation in questionnaire scores between schools reflect the proportion of ethnic minority students in each school? As we reported in Chapter 3, it was impossible to get exact information on the percentage of all ethnic minority students in most of the schools, mainly because of the embryonic state of ethnic monitoring. While the variations in questionnaire results did not appear to be due to the proportion of ethnic minority students in the schools there were, however, two factors relating to ethnicity which did seem significant. One was the difference in perception between students not from ethnic minority backgrounds, all ethnic minority students, and certain categories of ethnic and religious minority students — across the nine schools. The other was the *nature* of each school's ethnic profile: whether a school on the whole was 'bi-ethnic' or truly *multi*-ethnic seemed relevant both to the perceived state of inter-ethnic relationships and to a number of other contributory or criterial factors in those relationships.

We deal first with differences of perception between various 'categories' of student across the nine schools. Further analyses of the questionnaire data (see Table 4.1 for the raw scores) was carried out because of the richness and variety of interview responses — especially, though not exclusively, from ethnic and/or religious minority students. In interviews, most students in all but one of the schools described relationships as 'good' or 'quite good'. But in every school we were struck by the frequency with which a boy or girl would either insert a negative caveat in the context of describing relationships as generally good; or tell with evident feeling a particular story which presented a picture of unsatisfactory relationships. We were even more struck by the insight of some of the students we interviewed. It is worth repeating a remark made to us by a white year 10 girl at Yew School, which illustrates that combination of caution and insight rather well:

> There is some racism in school but the school needs to look more deeply
> to spot it. There are a few racists but they don't show their racism except
> maybe in name-calling. They know the school won't allow it.

At Ash School, where 88 per cent in the student questionnaire reported relationships to be satisfactory, a Hindu boy commented:

> In all schools you have one or two who cause problems. . . . But if any
> other school has a problem with racism this is the best place to come to
> see. They always get to the bottom of things here.

A girl at Fir School (over 90 per cent reporting satisfactory relationships in the questionnaire) qualified her estimate that relationships in the school were good by saying that there was some prejudice against Asian students:

> There is certainly bullying in certain years, but you do see Indian people
> walking down the street with white students getting along, and Greek
> students walking down the street with Indian and black students.

At Elm School (77 per cent reporting satisfactory relationships) a boy said that relationships were 'bearable — but we are on thin ice.' Another (Bangladeshi) student said that relationships were 'very poor' and added:

> The English hate Bengalis. Fights and name-calling happen a lot. They tell
> us to go back home and they push you around.

In more than one school students drew perceptive distinctions and connections between relationships inside and events outside the school. In Birch School, a year 8 girl commented 'It's not very good. There are gangs and fights, especially outside school.' Another student at the same school, who in interview described relationships at the school as quite good, said:

> Sometimes there are problems at the end of school. White students follow
> coloureds home, down the side streets.

At Pine (86 per cent reporting satisfactory relationships) a recent incident originating in the local community but with in-school effects was frequently mentioned by students. A white boy said 'Last term was an exception. It spoilt things with the Bengalis. It's not so easy now'. And a Bengali boy from Bangladesh went to some lengths to explain

> . . . social and geographical differences — and differences in religious practice which lead to squabbles and even fights. Sometimes it overflows into school.

A final illustration of the relationship between the general picture and particular perceptions comes from Oak School, where the score for satisfactory relationships in the student questionnaire was 91 per cent and students talked very positively on the whole about relationships. On the one hand, a Bengali boy said:

> Sometimes you might see a white girl going out with a black boy and I've got black friends in my class and I find them funny and good friends . . . I think they're all right to be with.

On the other hand, a Jewish boy commented:

> Most people in this school are racist. The whites are quiet about it. Generally the black people are really hard. They stick up for each other a lot. Whites are hard. Asians are regarded as sickly and weak. Although we do mix and talk to each other a lot . . . there's hostility.

It hardly needs saying that this and all other quotations from what students and teachers told us are reproduced in order to illuminate, not to furnish proof. This last comment, however, manages with remarkable economy to summarise views which were variously presented to us in interviews: the picture of whites as 'in control'; of Afro-Caribbeans as a solid and slightly menacing phalanx; of 'Asians' (sometimes differentiated, sometimes not) as vulnerable; and, generally, of underlying inter-ethnic tensions and hostility masked by surface tolerance and even sociability.

As pointed out earlier, the wealth of material from interviews, of which a small amount is reproduced here, led us to explore further the questionnaire data to see whether (as we had begun to suspect) it might confirm some differential experiences of inter-ethnic relationships between ethnic minority students in general and all others; between certain categories of ethnic minority and all others, and between a religious minority (Muslim) and all others. Tables 4.3 a and b gives the results for Question 9 analysed for just these combinations. As can be seen from the tables, when analysed by gender, the pattern for girls' and boys' responses was very similar, but there were significant differences between all ethnic minority students and others, and between Bangladeshi students and others. More ethnic minority students (10.7 per cent) than others (6.7 per cent) felt that students did not get on well, and ethnic minority students were less likely to choose the 'they get on very well' option (25.2 per cent) than others (31.9 per cent). This was particularly true of Bangladeshi students, only one in five (20.1 per cent) choosing that option.

Table 4.3a: Perception of inter-ethnic relationships, analysed by certain ethnic/religious categories, and by gender (all schools)

Q.9: How well do students from different backgrounds or religions get on with each other?

	All	Boys (1241)	Girls (1038)	Ethnic Minorities (1197)	All Others (1129)
They get on very well	28.5	29	28.3	25.2	31.9
They get on quite well	58.9	58.2	59.8	60	57.8
They don't get on well	8.8	8.7	8.5	10.7	6.7
They don't get on at all	2.3	3	1.6	2.3	2.4

Table 4.3b

	Muslims (492)	All Others (1834)	Bangladeshi (254)	All Others (2072)	Caribbean (153)	All Others (2173)
They get on very well	26.8	29	20.1	29.6	31.4	28.3
They get on quite well	60.8	58.4	64.2	58.3	61.4	58.7
They don't get on well	8.9	8.7	10.6	8.5	5.2	9.0
They don't get on at all	1.4	2.6	2	2.4	2.0	2.3

The results for students identifying themselves as Afro-Caribbean were also analysed. The contrast with both ethnic minority students in general and Bangladeshis in particular is interesting: 31.4 per cent of Afro-Caribbeans reported that students from different backgrounds in their schools got on 'very well', compared with 25.2 per cent of all ethnic minority students and 20.1 per cent of Bangladeshis; 61.4 per cent chose the 'quite well' option, which was not significantly different from those other groups. Afro-Caribbeans' responses were also rather more positive than those for the whole sample: 'very well' was chosen by 28.5 per cent of the whole sample and by 31.4 per cent of Afro-Caribbeans; 'quite well' by 58.9 per cent and 61.4 per cent respectively.

Before we leave this matter, it is interesting to reflect on the following irony: interviews tended to confirm the positive picture emerging from the questionnaire of Afro-Caribbeans' perceptions of relationships. Yet at every school in which there was a significant proportion of Afro-Caribbean students they were seen by some students and by some teachers as a source of disruption to good order and inter-ethnic harmony. Their characterisation by teachers as something of a school counter-culture was fairly pervasive, as was some students', and teachers', tendency to see them as threatening. It is not that that was the majority view in the schools; but only at Beech School did a different minority group (Bengalis) attract the same sort of negative comment — and not for quite the same reasons.

The issue of mismatch between Afro-Caribbean students and their schools has been extensively discussed in the literature, though not resolved. It is, of course, a subset of the general issue of the negative experiences of Afro-Caribbeans in British society. It raises the question of where correctly to locate the problem: in white racism *tout court*; in racism as a particular weapon of the class system; in the social legacy of colonialism; in British conservatism and xenophobia; in Afro-Caribbeans' alleged lack of supportive family structures (compared with the Asian communities in the UK); in Afro-Caribbeans' supposed lack of economic ambition; in the historical causes of that alleged lack of ambition — or in a combination of these and other possible factors. It is not our intention to go into the question here. But we can report that the issue, as exemplified in education, was live in the schools studied for this research. In schools (such as Yew, Ash, Fir, Oak) where the picture of inter-ethnic relationships presented to us was overwhelmingly positive, some interview responses suggested that, even in those schools, there were some who felt that harmony between Afro-Caribbean students and the school — as a social organisation, a rule-governed institution and as a community of learners — had yet to be achieved. As a teacher at Oak School commented:

> We haven't addressed the main problem, which is underachievement and exclusions of black students. Out of the last ten students excluded from school, nine were Afro-Caribbean boys. And I'm so aware of the number of black children who come to visit us after they've left school and express regret at the time they've wasted. We just haven't been able to motivate them.

And another (Afro-Caribbean) teacher at the same school:

> It should be acknowledged that Afro-Caribbeans tend to be noisy and exuberant; this shouldn't be treated as bad behaviour in itself. But misunderstandings do arise between them and white teachers — they've seen as being rude, but it's part of their culture.

Those remarks were made at a school where over 90 per cent of the students described inter-ethnic relationships as satisfactory or better; where over fifty first languages were spoken; where 95 per cent of students stayed on after 16, and the proportion of Afro-Caribbean students taking A levels was rising; and where there was constant, ubiquitous and public statement of commitment to equal opportunities.

Our interviews and discussions also led us to analyse the questionnaire data in terms of one religious minority (Muslim). Table 4.3b shows that the differences in the pattern between Muslims' and all others' reported perceptions were not significant. This would seem at first sight to be surprising, since we had gained the impression from interviews of some, perhaps disproportionate, disquiet felt by Muslim students about relationships in school. We cannot forget the comment of a year 10 girl at Oak School who described herself as 'English and Pakistani', about having had her religion ridiculed through jokes:

> We can't help it. We can't leave our religion. It makes me feel horrible. Sometimes I wished I shouldn't be a Muslim. Now I'm happy being a Muslim.

It was clear in that interview that, as she moved up through the school, things got better. Although in interviews we encountered some other similarly negative stories where religion was the focus, it must be remembered that the categories of self-description in the questionnaire allowed students multiple self-categorisation (so that a student could describe herself, for example, as English and Pakistani and Muslim — there were, in fact, many more complex self-descriptions than that in the questionnaire returns). It is obvious from Table 4.3b, and only to have been expected, that there were many more students describing themselves as Muslim than there were Bangladeshis. Many non-Bangladeshi Muslims were from families much longer-established in the UK than many of the Bangladeshi students.

To summarise: questionnaire and interview evidence, which were on the whole well-aligned, suggested that ethnic minority students had a less positive view of inter-ethnic relationships than others; that this was particularly true of Bangladeshi students (and, not surprisingly, of others from newly- or recently-arrived families such as refugees); that Afro-Caribbean students felt if anything more positively than students in general (though the feeling was not always reciprocated), and that membership of a religious minority as such did not materially affect the picture.

What *did* seem to affect the picture, however, was the degree of ethnic diversity in each of the nine schools. In the questionnaire the schools with the four lowest scores for the response: 'they get on very well' were Beech, Elm, Birch and Pine. Of those four schools, Beech, Elm and Pine had a substantial Bangladeshi community and Birch an equally substantial Gujarati community; in all cases the other large element was white Anglo-Saxon. The fact that three of the schools were in the northern sample is much less significant, we suggest than the fact that three of the five northern schools were mainly 'bi-ethnic' rather than multi-ethnic, and only one of the four southern schools. That demographic difference between the two groups of schools may indeed reflect differential settlement patterns in the UK, but, with only nine schools involved in the research it is impossible to make such a generalisation and the issue was in any case well beyond the scope of this study.

Earlier in this chapter we presented a comparative case study of Beech and Yew Schools, in which the contrast between the ethnic bipolarity of the former and the much greater diversity of the latter emerged as a salient point of comparison. That contrast holds good across the nine schools constituting the sample: analysis for the whole sample indicated that, while Bangladeshi students were less likely than all other students to select the 'very well' option (20.1 per cent against 29.6 per cent of all others and 28.5 per cent of whole sample), that proportion was still higher than in the three schools (Beech, Elm and Pine) with the large groups of Bangladeshi and white students, where the percentages in each school responding 'very well' were 11.5, 12.9 and 19.7 respectively. Birch, the school with the bipolarity of Gujarati Muslim and white students, also exhibited significant difference in perceived quality of relationships: 18.5 per cent chose the 'they get on very well' option against 28.5 per cent of the whole sample. Conversely, the schools with the richest ethnic diversity emerged with the most positive questionnaire responses in the 'very well' category: Yew (45.1 per cent); Fir (36.5 per cent); Larch (36.0 per cent); Ash (34.0 per cent) and Oak (30.9 per cent). All but one of these percentages were well above the average for all schools in the sample (28.5 per cent).

Many of the extracts from interviews and discussions with students and teachers already considered in this chapter have brought out the significance of the degree of ethnic diversity in the schools for their inter-ethnic relationships. But we may be in a position to consolidate the argument by reference to what teachers and students had to say about mixing between students of different backgrounds, and about the amount of inter-ethnic abuse on 'racial' or religious lines, in their schools. Those will be the detailed concern of Chapter 6. However, a number of references have been made in this chapter to examples of positive and negative interactions between students; their relevance to the quality of relationships in a school can hardly be doubted.

In sum, the quantitative data, interviews and discussions with students and teachers and our own observations convinced us that inter-ethnic relationships were better in the five relatively multi-ethnic, than in the bi-ethnic, schools. By 'better', we mean 'more harmonious, mutually tolerant, interactive, collaborative and friendly'. We do not necessarily mean that they were more free from any kind of conflict — though this was probably true of some of the schools as compared with some others.

In this chapter we have attempted a many-sided portrayal of inter-ethnic relationships in the nine schools, as perceived and reported by their teachers and students. Although discussion of final conclusions and suggested practical implications has been left to the last chapter, we have drawn attention to some interesting, suggestive and, perhaps, significant correlations. We summarise these now.

Firstly, the variety of perceptions illustrated above exemplify the complex nature of inter-ethnic relationships and the difficulty of characterising them coherently. Talking with some students during interviews, we sometimes found it hard to believe that they were all at the same school. Inevitably, students' perceptions depended largely on their first-hand experiences and the sub-cultures to which they belonged. Differences of perception did not simply follow ethnic differences. Internal differences of view were as common among teachers as among students; and in all schools there were some teachers who felt that the patterns of relationships were so complex that they were unwilling to be drawn into generalisation.

Secondly, it seemed evident that some schools were more 'powerful' than others in fashioning their own destinies and managing their internal and external relationships: the comparison between Beech and Yew Schools was the chosen, and only the most salient, case in point.

Thirdly, while there were *some* apparently regional variations in perceived quality of relationships, these were not thought in themselves to be significant. Significant differences did on the other hand emerge: ethnic minorities in general felt less positive than others; Bangladeshis even less so; Afro-Caribbeans more positive.

Fourthly, although it would be both simplistic and naive to suggest that relationships in any of the schools were *uniformly* better than in any other school, the weight of quantitative data and qualitative evidence strongly suggested that, the more multi-ethnic a school was, the better its relationships were felt to be.

Finally, on the question of inter-ethnic relationships as perceived by the respondents: questionnaire analysis and material from semi-structured interviews and informal discussions seemed on the whole to be mutually supportive. The use of both types of methodology has thus far enabled us to prepare the ground for further analysis of factors which we believe to be either crucial to, or criterial for, good relationships.

We have said little or nothing so far about what our research suggested to us concerning schools' handling of the curriculum — both formal and hidden; subject-based and otherwise; and about the relevance of curricular and cross-curricular issues to the quality of social relationships. We consider these matters in the next chapter.

Chapter 5

Inter-Cultural Knowledge, Equality and Relationships

Students' and Teachers' Inter-Cultural Knowledge and Understanding

It will be recalled that Chapter 3 set out some of our findings and impressions concerning (*inter alia*) what might be called the institutional knowledge-base for inter-ethnic relationships: the extent to which schools knew and understood their students' ethnicities, and the extent to which their staff were equipped by knowledge and experience to work effectively in schools in which ethnic diversity was a significant characteristic. This chapter explores a number of other perspectives on inter-cultural knowledge — as possessed by students and teachers — in the schools we studied: its perceived extent; the degree of importance attached to it by our respondents; its sources; the extent to which planned provision by the school was seen as influencing its growth (if at all), and the impact on relationships of provision targeted towards students of ethnic minority origin.

The questionnaire invited students to say how much they thought they knew about the beliefs and lifestyles of other students in their year group who belonged to communities or religious groups different from their own; and how much other students knew about them (see Appendix 3, Q6 and Q7). Students' level of claimed knowledge about others' cultures was modest, though not negligible. Over one-third (34.1 per cent) of students stated that they did not know very much; just under a third (32.8 per cent) felt that they knew 'quite a bit about most'. Nearly a quarter (23.7 per cent) felt confident that they knew 'a lot about most' or 'a lot about some'. However, during interviews, most of them expressed the view that they had learnt very little of what they did know as a result of planned transmission by the school. Teachers tended also to take a rather pessimistic view about what their schools were doing to transmit inter-cultural knowledge; a typical response by teachers was that what students did know was more likely to have been picked up by social contacts inside or outside the school than by deliberate efforts on the part of the school.

There were noticeable variations in students' perceptions of inter-cultural knowledge and understanding between different ethnic groups: more ethnic (and/ or religious) minority students than all other students claimed to know quite a bit or a lot about others' cultures. The questionnaire indicated that Muslim students were four times more likely than all other students to claim to know a lot about the cultures of most other student groups. Furthermore, on the whole, ethnic minority students reported that they knew more about others' cultures than others knew about theirs. More than four out of ten ethnic minority students felt that other students knew nothing or very little about their cultures — and for Afro-Caribbean students the proportion was almost half (48 per cent). That impression was reinforced by teachers' expressed views.

Those findings are, perhaps, not entirely surprising: no doubt it is true that members of ethnic minority groups in a society with a geography and history such as Britain has, are likely either to *be* more inter-culturally literate, or to behave as if they are, than their Anglo-Saxon fellow-citizens. The explanation for that would presumably lie on the one hand in the insularity and xenophobia of the white British; on the other hand, in ethnic minorities' necessary repertoire of survival and coping strategies in a society and culture not entirely theirs.

There was also considerable variation in students' perceptions between schools: more students in the northern schools felt they knew 'quite a bit' about others' cultures than those in the southern schools. There was also a strong tendency for northern students to report more positively than those in the south on the extent to which teachers helped them to understand other students' cultures. It is interesting to note, however, from our analysis of questionnaire responses, that these apparent regional variations did not correlate well with the overall quality of inter-ethnic relationships as perceived by students. For this and other reasons it is at least clear that levels of inter-cultural knowledge alone cannot determine the quality of inter-ethnic relationships.

When questioned about the school's role in transmitting a culture of cooperation and mutual respect between different ethnic groups, younger (year 8) students tended to respond vaguely, recalling specific inputs (for example in form periods; personal and social education lessons) only after prompting. Nearly all older (year 10) students had positive things to say, identifying either specific areas of the subject curriculum (particularly RE) or PSE-type lessons as the source of such input. We shall examine the role of curricular and cross-curricular activities in more detail a little later on.

It is impossible to generalise about even perceived views of students and teachers of the relationship between inter-cultural knowledge/understanding and inter-ethnic relationships in the schools studied — exemplifying the notoriously difficult problem of the relationship between knowledge and attitudes or behaviour in general. We have already seen that, according to the purely quantitative data, variations between schools in the reported extent of inter-cultural knowledge/understanding do not seem to correlate well with differences in the perceived quality of inter-ethnic relationships. Yet in all schools, between a quarter and a half of all teachers interviewed expressed the intuition that increased knowledge and understanding of each others' cultures was positively related to good relationships between students. Of these, most teachers interpreted 'inter-cultural knowledge' in terms of information about differences; but it is worth quoting again at least one — a science teacher — who emphasised the importance for inter-ethnic relationships of learning about cross-cultural universals:

(*through a course on genetics and inheritance*) the kids very much come to realise that we're all one species and we all function as humans in the same way and that group differences aren't that important when it comes to certain basic things.

Those teachers who were optimistic about the potential benefits of increased inter-cultural knowledge tended to base their view on intuition more than on specific examples. Our view, based on what we saw, is that some teachers are too close to their subject-matter and to their students to see the benefits actually happening: it is, perhaps, worth reflecting that not the least of the possible advantages of the 'action research' model of teachers' professional development is that it does challenge them to analyse practices — perhaps very good practices — which they otherwise either take for granted or consciously relate only to externally-imposed instrumental goals.

A variant of the intuitively-held view that planned knowledge input by the school helped inter-ethnic relationships was reference by some teachers in some schools to school ethos or philosophy. For some, this was a potent force; others put more emphasis on the limitations of planned transmission of inter-cultural knowledge and appropriate values by the school when set against the influences of home and the wider community:

We can give them a sense of equal value but translating it into the playground is another matter. Children suffer prejudice everywhere in society. It's a slow process to change the school so much.

Other teachers emphasised the importance of parental influences and of the condition of community relations in the school's catchment area. Their awareness of those influences were sometimes reinforced by our own perceptions. In this research we have consciously refrained from dealing substantially with the wider context of inter-ethnic relationships and have concentrated on in-school factors, largely because of limitations of time and resources. However, both in interviews with students and teachers and through our own observations we were reminded of the power of community factors in shaping relationships in school. On a number of occasions, as we have already seen, particular problems in the local community which had a 'racial' dimension seemed to be having a considerable, if short-term, impact on the quality of inter-ethnic life in the schools.

We noted earlier (Chapter 3) that students tended to see planned provision by the school as a limited source of knowledge and understanding of others' cultures, and that teachers often admitted their inter-cultural ignorance. There was, in fact, considerable variation between schools in the amount and quality of information provided on cultural diversity (for example through displays; multi-lingual information and resources; material on religions; resources supplied by local communities reflecting students' cultures; relevant publications in staffroom and library, etc.). That variation is to be seen against a dearth of professional development courses in aspects of ethnic diversity and their educational implications, across all of the schools. Interviews with teachers revealed that, while many of them were knowledgeable, experienced and sensitive in one relevant way or another, this was due much more to long experience of working in inner-city multi-ethnic and multi-faith situations, or to other relevant life experience, than to specific and substantial professional development in which learning more about students' cultural backgrounds was a major element. Overall, then, many teachers expressed a lack of sufficient knowledge of their students' cultural backgrounds. It is therefore not surprising that on the whole students tended to see their own inter-cultural knowledge as arising more from life than from planned school provision.

Although the impact of knowledge on relationships is generally unproven (see, for example, Bullivant, 1987), and in the context of this research remained so, questions may be posed about curricula in multi-ethnic schools which are pertinent to this research. For example, the way the curriculum is organised and delivered, and the way in which learning material is selected, may *reflect* other aspects of the quality of school life which bear on, or are evidence for, the quality of inter-ethnic relationships.

The Relevance of Curricular and Cross-Curricular Provision

Teachers' perceptions of the curriculum as part of a school's response to cultural diversity were undoubtedly affected by the impact of National Curriculum requirements, which at the time of the research were engaging teachers in new, time-consuming and often bureaucratic tasks. An additional factor shaping approaches to a curriculum sensitive to cultural diversity was the particular situation of certain schools at the time — for example, reorganisation involving the introduction of ethnic minority students in sizeable numbers; newness, and transfer (while the researchers were in the school) from ILEA to a new borough authority. A third factor which seemed relevant to many aspects of inter-ethnic relationships, and which apparently affected teachers' perceptions of an appropriate curriculum, was the ethnic make-up of the schools studied: some of the teachers in schools which in the main had a large proportion of *one* ethnic minority group, talked about the undesirability of a merely 'bi-ethnic' curriculum, and stressed the importance of a global perspective. That view highlights the issue of whether a curriculum for cultural diversity should be based on the rationale of reflecting the ethnic composition of a school and neighbourhood or whether the rationale should be independent of local demography.

As well as the constraints mentioned above, there seemed to be the additional negative factor, already mentioned, of teachers' lack of personal inter-cultural knowledge and professional development opportunities in this area. We have already seen (in Chapter 3) that in the nine schools studied teachers' recent experience of explicit professional development related to ethnic diversity was very sparse; and their initial training had in most cases been largely devoid of such material (that is not to deny, of course, the substantial *informal* and work-based experience which many teachers had had). Other research confirms this picture (see, for example,

Wright, 1992 and, in relation to physical education, Carroll and Hollinshead, 1993). We see the relative paucity of systematic and relevant professional development in this area encountered among teachers in these nine multi-ethnic schools as a cause for concern.

All teachers interviewed, however, felt that the curriculum *should* play a role in contributing to students' knowledge of other cultures than their own. They varied in their judgment of the degree to which their own subjects were contributing. There were equivalent variations in all schools between curriculum areas — this was evident from curriculum documentation supplied to the researchers, as well as from teachers' responses. There was near-unanimity among teachers across the schools on the potential of arts and humanities subjects for fostering inter-cultural knowledge and understanding, and (as we shall see) evidence of *practical* recognition of that potential. In a minority of cases teachers reported on the inclusion of inter-cultural and non-Eurocentric perspectives in mathematics and science syllabuses.

Senior staff in all schools seemed committed to the principle of a curriculum for cultural diversity. Some supported their statements in specific ways: 'Wherever there are options offered in exam syllabuses, all our departments have chosen non-European ones where possible.' It has to be said, however, that in certain schools a considerable proportion of teachers interviewed displayed a sceptical attitude towards their senior managements' professed commitment to multi-cultural/anti-racist education and equal opportunities in general. There were wide variations of perception here both between and within schools. It was clear to the researchers that some senior managements were the driving force behind curriculum and other initiatives related to inter-ethnic relationships and other aspects of equal opportunity. Some, on the other hand, were seen by *some* members of their staffs as concerned more with containing potential sources of conflict than with energetic promotion of equal opportunities policy and practice. There is no easy judgment to be made here; but we did gain the impression that the more multi-ethnic the school and the composition of its staff, the more we were likely to hear polarised views among the staff about the extent to which senior managers were serious about equal opportunities, multi-cultural curricula and confronting racism. It might be said that in some cases senior managers' recognition of the multi-cultural curriculum imperative, possibly genuine in itself, was diluted by their remoteness from the details of curriculum delivery and by their need to manage large staffs with — in some cases — very diverse attitudes, cultural and ideological backgrounds and educational/ political priorities. Perhaps, therefore, their practical commitment to the relevant curriculum responses was sometimes seen by some of their junior colleagues rather as devotion to motherhood and apple pie.

Approaches to designing, within the obvious constraints, a curriculum for cultural diversity ranged from explicit coverage of racism-related issues, such as colonialism in history syllabuses, to enhancement of ethnic self-consciousness through projects examining students' own ethnicities and community roots, to in-direct processes such as relevant criteria for choice of literature in English sylla-buses. Drama lessons sometimes involved role play aimed at challenging stereotypes. Craft and design curricula in one school were seen by the Head of Faculty as an opportunity for relating some important artistic processes to their cultural roots, for example bronze casting and the Benin civilisation. Mathematics and science curricula — though unevenly across the schools — were sometimes informed by the desire to avoid Eurocentrism by stressing the variety of cultural origins of important mathematical systems and scientific/technological discovery and innovation. Language awareness courses were being developed in at least two of the schools, aimed at bringing all students to a better understanding of language as such, and an acceptance of the validity of community languages in particular. Only in one of the schools did the course seem to be gaining some popularity with students.

In music, insofar as syllabuses were driven by awareness of cultural diversity (and, it has to be said, this was only so in a few schools) two approaches stood out: one, relatively familiar, approach was to recognise and incorporate the various cultural traditions students brought with them as these were exemplified in music. The other, more interesting because less familiar, was to deal with major musical traditions other than western 'classical' *as music*, and not just as examples of 'other cultures to be celebrated'; that is to say, with the emphasis on common principles governing all music, rather than on cultural difference. This is an example of a distinction our sense of whose importance has been reinforced by this research: it is the distinction between cultural imperialism (*the western European, or 'British', way is the right way*) and cultural universalism (*look for cross-cultural universals of, and equivalences in, human experience*). The former is to be opposed; the latter to be (cautiously) embraced.

Interviews with teachers revealed that, for some, strategies and styles of curriculum delivery mattered as much as, or more than, content. Group work and other student-centred approaches were seen as helping to foster better relationships, though not many particular examples were offered. Specific mention was made (more by students than teachers) of *cross*-curricular, 'process-oriented' work such as form tutor periods and personal and social education programmes. As mentioned above, older students tended to see the relevance to good relationships of discussion of appropriate issues taking place in PSE and equivalent lessons. Students also cited the opportunities for discussion of ethical and other relevant issues, and for learning about the religious dimension of 'other' cultures, presented by RE programmes. But there was considerable variety of perception here, as there was of what RE was trying to do, as between different schools and different students in the same school. Although some students saw RE as enabling them to learn about others' lifestyles, others saw it as confined to teaching only about 'other religions' and as failing to impart broader cultural knowledge. Still others (a minority) actually resented what they saw as RE's over-preoccupation with pluralism. Across the nine schools, there was a marked tendency for RE as such to disappear from the educational diet by the year 10.

The publication in 1994 of the government's new guidelines on the balance and content of religious education in maintained schools has reinforced the policy of making RE predominantly Christian in character (first articulated during the passage of the 1988 Education Reform Act). For a host of reasons, this latest intervention renders even more problematic the potential role of RE in positively influencing inter-ethnic relationships. The muddled thinking which the new policy betrays on, for example, what a religious education in a non-denominational school might be *for*, is likely only to restrict, rather than enhance, that role. That is to say nothing at all about the effects of the imposed teaching in multi-ethnic schools *of* Christianity (rather than *about* it as one among several important exemplars of religious and moral experience as such). If the genesis, development and current overhaul of the National Curriculum as a whole give little comfort to those who think that education for ethnic and cultural diversity is important, the recent history of government interventions in the RE curriculum is a particularly sad example. The fact that these interventions are likely to be ineffective is only a partial source of comfort.

The question of the *impact* of the curriculum on inter-ethnic relationships is, of course, a refinement of the more general problem — already mentioned — of the relationship between knowledge and attitudes/behaviour. Teachers were able to give (and we saw) a number of specific examples of curricular practice where there was a clear intention to put increased knowledge at the service of better relationships. There is certainly a sense of the term 'understanding' which makes it cognate to such terms as 'empathy', 'sympathy', or even 'cooperation'. So it seems a fair bet that, in some way, increased inter-cultural knowledge *must* lead to increased understanding in the sense just described, and thence to better relationships. Most teachers seemed implicitly to hold this *a priori* view, as exemplified by this senior teacher:

> (*Accurate information and increased awareness lead*) to students making informed decisions. It's no good preaching at children but we do need to present them with factual knowledge which should help to build good relationships.

Occasionally, a definite and positive impact on relationships was claimed by teachers for particular curriculum projects or units within syllabuses. Research of a longitudinal kind would have to be done, perhaps, to see how sustained such impact might be. Some teachers, though uncertain about the direct impact of multi-cultural/anti-racist curricula, nevertheless asserted their value in, among other things, raising the level of self-esteem of minority students. (We saw no evidence that this contention had been systematically investigated through classroom-based research.) Examples also presented themselves of determined and sustained efforts to involve certain minority groups in curriculum activities seen by the teachers as education-ally worthwhile and beneficial as far as relationships were concerned, even where responses by students and parents were sometimes unfavourable because of in-fringement of cultural/religious taboos. This illustrates a classic dilemma, and one which often surfaces in a plural society: should people be forced to be free?

In all schools, the majority of students said that they learnt very little in lessons about how different groups of people in Britain lived. A somewhat higher proportion, though still a minority, said that they learnt something in lessons about the world outside Britain. Most students seemed not to be conscious of curricular aims of imparting world perspectives or awareness of cultural diversity in Britain. However, although the direct impact of curriculum content and processes of delivery on inter-ethnic relationships remains open to question, it nevertheless seems certain that curriculum and relationships are at least correlated, in the sense that one of the central ways in which a school may be seen to be consciously *addressing* the issue of inter-ethnic relationships is through curriculum activities. The extent to which development of knowledge and values appropriate to good relationships is addressed across the faculties and departments of a school, and not only in isolated areas or only by enthusiastic individual teachers, at least reflects the extent to which there is a whole-school approach to the issue of relationships. In some of the nine schools studied there seemed to be a high level of consciousness of the importance of inter-ethnic relationships and equal opportunities in general, and this was reflected across the curriculum. In others, the picture was much more fragmented, and curriculum responses to cultural diversity were relatively dependent on individual initiative.

The Role of Extra-Curricular Activities

Interviews with teachers and students convinced the researchers of the importance of this dimension of the life of the school for inter-ethnic relationships. Although most teachers put 'fair and equal treatment of students' at the top of their list of *non*-curricular ways in which they could contribute to good relationships, some put considerable emphasis on extra-curricular activities. The prevailing view among teachers was that involvement by ethnic minorities in these activities entailed informal contact with other students and with staff and thus promoted good relationships.

The pattern emerging from interviews (including those with students) was that, while certain ethnic minority groups were reasonably represented in certain kinds of activity, Muslim students were under-represented. In sport, the non-participation of Asian students in general and Muslims in particular was noticeable. In one school with a large proportion of South Asian students, a PE teacher observed:

> Hindu students are more likely to be involved. Muslims go to mosque in the evening and lunchtime is already full of activities. Many Asian students don't seem to have an interest in sport. The white kids feel that they don't join in.

However, another teacher felt that part of the problem lay with the school, commenting that some Asians were good at sports such as table tennis which were not drawn on by the school. This example of not apparently exploiting Asians' talent in a particular sport is instructive. The same may be said of how a school seeking to involve ethnic minorities in drama and other performances goes about choosing what to put on. We recall how, at one of the two schools used for the pilot study which preceded this research (a highly multi-ethnic school), that year's school play was largely written by the students; was on the theme of migration and the consequences of UK legislation; told the story of the difficulties of a Cypriot family in that context, and cast its characters right across the ethnic profile of the school. It was, for example, not seen as in any way extraordinary that an Afro-Caribbean girl played one of the central (Cypriot) characters, in a school in which one of the largest ethnic minority groups was Greek Cypriot — because she was a talented actor. That contrasts with the example of the choice of Bugsy Malone in one of the schools studied in this project — a musical in which the image of women is such as to be offensive to many Muslims; not surprisingly, very few of the large number of Muslim students in the school participated or attended performances.

Our evidence supports views held by many staff that Muslim girls were not involved in social activities outside school. Although such lack of involvement was seen by some staff as illustrating a repressive home situation, it should be said that girls often did not give this impression in interviews, often speaking positively of their preferences to be involved in home-based activities. Of course, cultural and religious expectations may have a persuasive psychological effect. Perhaps more significant is the lack of involvement of most of the Muslim girls interviewed in school activities. Explanations lie partly in the fact that activities involving girls staying behind after school or going away were said to be unacceptable to Muslim parents who were concerned about the welfare of their girls (in the case of Muslim boys it was mosque attendance which kept them from being involved). In addition, a high proportion of school extra-curricular activities were related to sport and the general interest in sporting activities was much lower among Asian pupils, particularly Muslims. Finally, often other high profile extra-curricular activities were related to music and drama, not areas in which Muslim girls are likely to be involved. None of this is surprising and is supported by Smith and Tomlinson's research in which analysis of pupil attendance by ethnicity showed Asian pupils less involved than English and analysis by religion showed Muslims as less involved than Hindus or Sikhs (Smith and Tomlinson, 1989).

Overall, ethnic minority students were under-represented in extra-curricular participation, with Muslim girls the most likely not to take part. If such involvement and informal contact with other students and staff is as effective as many teachers argued in promoting good inter-ethnic understanding and relationships then the low level of participation by Asian students is likely to lessen the impact of attempts to develop a whole school response to cultural diversity. Unfortunately, evidence presented by most teachers indicated that the number and scope of extra-curricular activities in schools are in decline. Furthermore, there is evidence that patterns of difficulty of involvement in such activities are already developing in primary schools (Wright, 1992).

A recent study (Verma and Darby, 1994) explored the relationship between ethnicity, culture and gender on the one hand and participation in sport and recreation on the other. The study focused on a number of factors having a bearing on the participation in any kind of sporting or physical activity by people from ethnic minority communities. One of the focal points was to explore the factors peculiar to ethnic minority groups which might inhibit or encourage participation in sport

:isure. The findings confirmed many small-scale studies as well as our
..w that schools with even well-developed equal opportunity policies are
unlikely to increase participation in sport by ethnic minorities, particularly by Asian
girls, unless they take into account their students' cultural traditions and religious
beliefs.

A people's culture is a powerful force in their lives. It helps to define their
personal as well as group identities. It is also a very lasting force. Modes of thought
and behaviour derived from the socialisation process are deeply rooted in a group
or individual's self perception. These should not be lightly rejected so that they can
be replaced by socially more convenient and acceptable alternatives.

School Responses to Minority Needs

During interviews, students sometimes expressed views about attempts made by
their schools to respond to the particular needs or requirements of ethnic and
religious minority students. Comments were often positive, particularly when expressed by minority students who felt that their school was making genuine efforts
to respond to felt or perceived needs. Negative experiences tended to focus on
school dinners (which often came in for criticism for their failure to respond creatively to religious requirements or cultural cuisine), provision for religious minorities and the occasional mention of a lack of provision for a minority language within
the timetabled subjects (although other students explained that they would not take
advantage of such provision even if it existed).

White students rarely commented on minority provision; when they did, this
often reflected a quite different perception: that the school, in its preferential treatment of minority students, was being unfair to others. For example, a white student
in Fir School felt that the school had 'tried too hard and given them ("blacks")
more rights so the blacks are into black superiority which makes whites not like
them.' In Beech School, a school with a large proportion of Asian students, an
Afro-Caribbean student felt the same way: 'The Bengali students get special treatment. African, Chinese and Spanish don't get special treatment at all. The teaching
standard has to be lowered because of all the students not speaking English.' White
students sometimes commented on the way in which minority students were able
to do or wear things which they couldn't. In schools where only Muslim girls were
allowed to wear trousers, other girls often felt that this was unfair. A girl in Elm
School disliked it when 'quite a few of the coloured girls come to school with quite
a lot of make-up on and large earrings and they don't get done for it, but most of
the time if we did this we would get told off'.

Attempts were also made to assess the degree of response made by schools to
the felt or perceived linguistic, religious and cultural requirements of minority
students. In interviews, teachers were asked if the school made any particular
provision for students from minority ethnic, linguistic or religious backgrounds
and, if so, whether they felt such provision helped or hindered good relationships.
The degree to which schools responded to these needs varied across the sample. In

all but one school, where most teachers felt that the school had made slow progress in responding to minority needs, teachers reported that their schools were taking such needs seriously and developing appropriate responses. However, in all schools, the philosophical and practical problems associated with such responses were often raised. These problems can best be described in terms of a series of tensions. The first kind of tension was between responding to the specific needs of minority students and preserving a philosophy of treating all children in the same way (a specific case of the issue, first made explicit by Aristotle, of the injustice which can arise from treating unequals equally). Some teachers did express the view that same treatment might have to have priority over treatment according to specific need, where the preservation of harmony was at a premium, and where minority students might be seen as receiving preferential treatment. Many teachers observed how responses to minority needs might lead to resentment by white students (and even staff) unless accompanied by clear explanations and ongoing inter-ethnic education. Although we had reservations about the motivations of some of our respondents in this area of discussion, we were reminded of one of the main findings of the MacDonald Report (MacDonald, 1989) on the Burnage High School tragedy: that over-exclusive concentration on the perceived needs of minorities, without proper communication and consultation with the majority, helped to create the right climate for the violent expression of white resentment.

The second tension was between providing opportunities or facilities which strengthened minority community identity and the danger of increasing separatism. This is well illustrated by examples given of clubs and societies aimed directly at minority students (for example, a Muslim prayer club) or indirectly (for example, Bengali language classes or an Indian film society). While such provisions were often described by teachers as strengthening minority students' self-esteem and sense of belonging to the school, they were also seen by some as contributing to the polarising of communities.

Thirdly, there was in some situations a tension between what might be perceived (by teachers, LEAs, parents, etc.) as appropriate provision for minority students and the felt needs of students themselves. This stemmed sometimes from the failure of such groups to recognise the vast range of individual stances taken by students in relation to their religious, linguistic or cultural background. In one school with a large percentage of Muslim students, pressure had been brought by the local Muslim community to make 'Muslim dress' *compulsory* for Muslim students. In other schools, the provision of language courses in minority languages was reported as not popular among minority students, who saw them as of little interest or of no career value.

Language Provision

The main 'special' provision mentioned by teachers in all schools was English as a Second Language (E2L). Most schools provided some language support for parents at parents' evenings or used translating services from time to time for letters or newsletters. However, often schools depended on the goodwill of teachers or others who spoke minority languages, rather than on an LEA support service. In one school, interpretation was provided by a laboratory technician and was described as inappropriate by some teachers, who felt that the LEA ought to provide this service.

Of the nine schools, the most comprehensive provision for *mother tongue* teaching was in Larch School, where Greek, Turkish and Italian were taught on the main school timetable within the modern languages department. In Beech School, Bengali and Greek were offered for GCSE, and Greek lessons were available after school. In most other schools, language options were available, but to a lesser extent. In schools where provision was made, levels of take-up by students were often low, teachers often commenting on these language options being seen as 'poor relations', because of under-resourcing. In Fir School, Gujerati and Turkish had been provided by peripatetic teachers in the past but were no longer available. Reasons given for this were the alleged unreliability of staff (a comment made in two other schools about peripatetic minority language teachers) and the lack of popularity of the options among students, who did not see them as career options. In other schools, language teachers spoke of the difficulty of finding qualified teachers, or of recruiting viable groups.

Religion

The second most frequent area of response to minority students was towards religious needs, particularly of Muslim students. Teachers from all schools spoke about the importance of respecting religious beliefs and practices. However, the nature and range of practical responses to minority religious needs varied substantially. In most schools, assemblies tended to be broadly Christian, with some recognition of other faiths, particularly at festival times. This was especially true of Yew School, which was a Church of England aided school. However, in two schools, teachers described assemblies as not being religious at all. In Fir School, for example, the headteacher felt that assemblies should be about 'sensitising all to diversity' and were moral rather than religious in content. In Beech School, one teacher described the school's response to religion as 'conflict avoidance'. There was no worship in school assembly, though festivals might be acknowledged.

In schools with a large percentage of Muslim students, the matter of provision of a room for prayer often arose. Here, as in so many other contexts, we encountered much diversity of opinion and of practice. Several teachers in one school commented that prayer facilities were made on an *ad hoc* basis (for example, teachers allowing their own formrooms to be used at lunchtimes) but many commented that the school ought to have a clearly defined room for prayer. In another school, specific provision had been made for prayer (although staff varied in their assessment of how much this was used). A Muslim 'prayer club' was reported in one of the schools, although here it was also observed that interest on the part of Muslims had lapsed. We discovered an arrangement in one school whereby students were allowed to attend mosque on Fridays. Several teachers suggested that such pro- vision should be kept 'low key' so that differences were not emphasised. Others were not in favour of schools making such provision because it was divisive. However, teachers at one of the schools commented that the absence of a prayer room meant that Muslim students went home at lunchtime; providing one would encourage them to stay and mix more.

Schools also generally responded sympathetically to Muslim students' particu- lar circumstances during Ramadan. This ranged from an 'overlooking' of absences during Eid to a full formal and published policy on Ramadan. In Pine School, con- cern was expressed by some teachers at the resentment felt by non-Muslim students who did not get these holidays, and there was some discussion about closing the school on such occasions.

In all schools the dietary needs of minority students were acknowledged, but this usually went no further than providing a vegetarian option in the canteen. In all schools, most teachers talked about trying to respond creatively to religious traditions and prohibitions. For example, in Yew School PE staff mentioned that showers were not made compulsory for Muslim students, although health education was used to explain the value of them. In Elm School staff often quoted an example of a Muslim girl who had arrived recently and wanted to wear a headscarf. This was allowed, although after a short time she stopped wearing it. In Pine School, requests from some Muslim parents for students not to use alcohol in science experiments had received a favourable response. However, there were some teachers who were less sympathetic to such responses, such as an art teacher who observed that there had been no requests from Muslim parents with regard to representational art and added 'I would react negatively if there were — art has nothing to do with religion'.

Teachers were asked if they were aware of any particular requests made by minority communities. In almost all schools, the only teachers who felt able to comment on whether or not such requests had been made were senior management. All schools which reported such requests argued that they tried to respond, usually successfully. Most issues were to do with dress, translation of documents and matters to do with games and PE. Although most teachers were in favour of their school responding to the felt or perceived needs of minority students, there was also a degree of ambivalence. The tensions mentioned above, between minority needs and general expectations, were often alluded to in one way or another. Language support was almost always seen as a welcome response and was often described as making minority students more self-confident and improving their self-esteem. Teachers often spoke highly of E2L teachers and language support staff. However, even in this area teachers in one school argued that the presence of bilingual teachers was a barrier because white students did not regard them as 'proper teachers'.

Positive responses to religious diversity were not always welcomed by stu- dents. A deputy head observed that an assembly about Eid 'had given the Bang- ladeshis a positive identification, but the more stroppy white kids had refused to touch the sweets made by the Bangladeshi girls'. A Chinese student in one school commented that although Asian girls were allowed to dress in their own traditional clothes on 'non-uniform days', Asian girls tended not to wear saris 'because they get called "curtains" — so they stay at home instead.' There was often a fear of resentment developing, despite attempts to explain clearly to students why certain practices were adopted. Occasionally, the temptation by minority students to 'play the system' (for example, with regard to wearing whatever clothes they wanted) was also mentioned. Several senior staff highlighted the importance of trying to incorporate responses to particular needs within the overall policy of the school — for example, allowing not just Muslim girls but all girls to wear trousers. Many teachers expressed the hope that short-term problems would be overcome as students became used to the idea of the school responding *differently* but *fairly* to students, particularly if provision was accompanied by explanations and firmness.

It was not the intention of the research to conduct a full investigation into special provision for minority students, but rather to examine whether such provision helped or hindered inter-ethnic relationships. The examples given above illustrate the dilemma of the multi-ethnic school: unless the school community is to be no more than a collection of separate sub-communities based on religion or ethnicity, then all students must experience a minimum level of shared activities, experiences and values. On the other hand, if pluralism is taken seriously, the school will consider the maximum extent to which it may recognise and value ethnic and religious differences. While this tension raises a range of issues to do with resources, community values, vested interests and teacher awareness, the key issue for the present study relates to how different groups of students perceive the school's responses in the light of their own sense of fairness. In view of the fact that even some teachers felt that simple 'same treatment' was the only safe stance for the school to adopt, it was understandable that many students found a more sophisticated response based on individual needs, beliefs and practices hard to handle. While there will always be some students who feel badly treated by the system, the majority we spoke to during this study were sensitive to minority needs, particularly in relation to language or religious practices. However, when they felt that minority students were allowed to 'get away with things' or benefit from rules which could just as easily be extended to all students, there was more likely to be a sense of injustice and a temptation to take it out on other students rather than the system. As was mentioned above, several teachers spoke of attempts to incorporate as many responses to minority needs as possible within general school rules. In one school where school uniform had become a key issue, a new school policy was developed based partly on the canvassed views of all students. Clearly, schools need to be just as concerned about seeking ownership of school policies by students, as by staff.

Whatever the impact of the formal and hidden curriculum on inter-ethnic relationships in the schools we studied may have been — and it is impossible to make categorical judgments here — there can be no doubt about the relevance of evidence concerning the nature of student-student and teacher-student interactions — both positive and negative; reported and observed. In Chapter 4 we necessarily included some material of this kind as part of our synoptic review of the perceived quality of relationships. In the next chapter we return to the subject of those interactions, focusing in some detail on the descriptive and explanatory evidence concerning inter-ethnic mixing (or its absence); and on patterns of inter-ethnic abuse.

Chapter 6

Sociability, Indifference and Hostility

In this chapter we examine the evidence from our study concerning patterns of inter- and intra-ethnic grouping and the factors which influenced them; various kinds of abuse between students on 'racial' or ethnic lines; the roles, attitudes and behaviour of teachers, and the ways in which schools acted and reacted in these contexts.

Inter- and Intra-Ethnic Grouping

In interviews with students, this subject was introduced by asking them about their close friends in and out of school. The responses revealed significant variation between schools: in one highly multi-ethnic school (Oak) most students said that their 'close friends' came from other ethnic groups than their own. This was not untypical of the more ethnically diverse schools in the sample. Patterns of stronger intra-ethnic preference tended to emerge in the 'bi-ethnic' schools. Across the schools, expressed reasons for cross-ethnic friendships tended to be shared interests and attitudes, and mutual trust. A striking example is provided by the year 10 boy who had described himself as 'Hindu and Asian', and who told us about his African and Chinese best friends:

> We all get along — go to the same plays; all like sports.

Similarly, a white boy (from a different school) said that his closest friends

> . . . tend to like football and sport. Some are Asian and some are black. It's not a case of other races.

Although on the whole evidence of *intra*-ethnic preference in terms of reported close friendships outweighed the *inter*-ethnic kind, the picture we gained from interviews was balanced by many clear examples of cross-ethnic friendship. The most likely sources of statements of strong intra-ethnic preference were Muslim student groups in bi-ethnic schools, where security, mutual support and gender were the most commonly-expressed criteria for choice of friends.

Outside school, reported cross-ethnic close friendships were less common, though fairly frequent. The difference between the patterns of preference in and out of school raises the question of the nature and significance of 'close friendships' as defined by students. It is, of course, not surprising that, in a community well-defined in terms of ethnicity, girls and boys are more likely to draw their friends from the same ethnic group than would be the case in school. We did not ask students whether they saw any difference in what *counted* as a close friendship as between their relationships in school and those out of school. However, we did wonder whether, in talking about 'close friendships' in school, students all meant the same thing. Furthermore, bearing in mind the defining characteristics of schools as institutions — in particular, their socialising purposes, we are not convinced that 'close friendships' *as such* are necessarily an indicator of the quality of inter-ethnic relationships in a school. As students move up the school, 'close friends' change with sometimes bewildering rapidity. Convivial social contact goes on all the time, quite separately from the emotionally-charged episodes of making and breaking 'best' friendships. On reflection, we believe that *mixing* is more significant for this study than friendship. As we have seen, the criteria which students tended to express for choice of what they *called* 'close friends' in school ranged from shared interests and attitudes to security, mutual support and own-gender preference. That suggests that removing barriers to social contact matters more than monitoring the incidence of cross-ethnic 'close friendships'.

Students were given the opportunity to talk about the factors which they saw as militating against mixing across ethnic groups. Teachers' perceptions were also solicited. Most students reported factors such as age and school organisation (banding, setting) as the most important negative factors. Teachers tended to draw attention to the influence of communal segregation outside the school. In schools (and these tended to be the bi-ethnic more than the multi-ethnic schools) where cross-ethnic mixing was relatively limited, white students reporting social contact with Asians often picked out those Asian students who were seen as more integrated into the dominant (white) culture. That seemed to suggest that, in such cases, what happened in school reflected rather than shaped relationships outside the school between newer settlers and the dominant culture. Reluctance to mix with certain groups was reported by some students as based on fear — for example, of gangs dominated by Afro-Caribbean boys, or fear of racist hostility on the part of white students. Conversely, one school presented strong (though not unique) evidence that Afro-Caribbean students felt excluded from the school's overt culture, and formed in-groups for mutual support — thus reinforcing the tendency for some students and teachers to feel threatened by them; while some white students in most of the schools expressed the view that Asians were reluctant to mix with them because of peer pressure to stay in their group. In two schools (Elm and Beech), both somewhat ethnically polarised, there was a tendency for white students to see Asians (Bengalis) as the dominant group, and thus to report feeling threatened. It was striking, but consistent with our findings in other areas of our research, that even where students reported that relationships were not bad, those in bi-ethnic schools tended implicitly to adopt a 'negative' model of good relationships (defined implicitly in terms of absence of overt hostility). That view was typified by a fifth year boy at Birch School:

Things are OK because we keep away from each other. Keeping to ourselves is best.

In those schools with essentially bi-ethnic communities the tendency to polar-
ise in the playground was more likely to be reflected in the classroom than was the
case in the relatively diverse schools. For example, in one school a discussion
group of year 10 students, which was ethnically mixed but contained no students
from the large Bangladeshi group in school, argued that there was a high degree
of separation in classes:

> (White Boy) . . . if you walk into any class, right, it's usual you'll see a
> Paki there (points), a couple of Pakis over there in that corner. They'll stay
> to themselves because they know once you start to mix, there's bound to
> be an argument and when there's an argument between a white person and
> a Bengali . . . the only way to solve it . . .

> (Chinese girl) . . . is to sit apart!

Not surprisingly, inter-ethnic mixing was much more common in the more ethnically diverse schools. The typical picture in such schools, emerging from interviews with students and teachers and from our own observations, was one in which
observed classroom grouping tended to be determined far more by gender than by
ethnicity. Very few examples were observed in lessons of blacks sitting next to
blacks or Asians sitting next to Asians — and there seemed to be nothing
unspontaneous about the cross-ethnic groupings. Observed groupings away from
the classroom exhibited the same tendency. Students in the more ethnically diverse
schools often expressed the view that it was impossible not to mix, both inside and
outside the classroom.

It may seem obvious that the degree of mixing between students of different
ethnicities in a school is positively connected with the quality of inter-ethnic relationships; but that was not the unanimous view of the teachers. A teacher at Birch
School justified intra-ethnic grouping in this way:

> The ideal of the school is that it would be a better quality community if
> they mixed together more. But they tend to group because of their com-
> mon ground. People should be proud of their heritage.

At Pine School, a teacher said: '. . . We all find our own friends. Why should we
force things?' Such remarks typify the attitude of a number of teachers in schools
where intra-ethnic grouping was more common than cross-ethnic mixing. On the
other hand, teachers in the same and other schools did feel that interaction between
groups was indeed important to the quality of school life, pointing to examples of
large-scale 'herding' (as one teacher put it) of students of a particular ethnic group
as threatening to other students and even teachers. In the two schools in which there
was a numerical (and increasing) majority of Bengali Muslim students (Beech and

Pine) some teachers expressed strong concern at that numerical dominance. In one of the schools, several teachers saw the growing proportion of (mainly) Bengali students as the main cause of a decrease in cross-ethnic mixing. Another teacher saw it as posing a threat to inter-ethnic harmony. At both of these schools, a considerable number of teachers expressed unease about the perceived degree of demographic polarity along ethnic, and in some cases linguistic, lines, and saw it as causing polarisation in inter-ethnic relationships:

> If we had a better balance in each class (mixing) would tend to happen more naturally. In a way it can be quite unhelpful because if you take certain classes, some of the local grown products are two or three in maybe twenty-five, so they probably feel they've been taken over . . . So in a way I think it can be quite unhelpful having so many kids of a particular ethnic origin in a group.

The Burnage Report (MacDonald, 1989) argued that the prevalence of intra-ethnic grouping in Burnage School was itself a symptom of underlying racism. Yet comments such as that quoted immediately above (typical of many which were made to us) must also be viewed with some suspicion, even though they are plur-alist on the surface. It would be tempting, but inappropriate, to discuss at this stage the possible underlying motives or policy implications of such remarks — except to say that, if they reflect negative inter-ethnic attitudes, then they are themselves a negative factor in inter-ethnic relationships; and if they tend to arise (as they did) only in the bi-ethnic schools, then our contention that the perceived quality of relationships tended to vary in proportion to the degree of ethnic diversity in the school is to that extent vindicated. In any case, that quotation contrasts interestingly with the words from a teacher at Birch School, quoted earlier, about the need for pride in one's heritage.

Thus, except in situations where the grouping of students by ethnicity was perceived as a threat (to other students or even teachers) there was no unanimous view about its impact on the quality of inter-ethnic relationships. While many teachers said that they intuitively felt that more mixing by students was to be preferred, they saw no real problems with students choosing to be with others with whom they shared cultural, linguistic or religious interests.

Few teachers tried to enforce inter-ethnic mixing in lessons, but many gave examples of ways in which they tried to encourage it, particularly in group work and in activities such as drama and sport. Factors affecting inter-group mixing are, of course, complex. At one level, the degree of mixing may be formally controlled by a dominant community. In school, the ultimate control of formal situations is in the hands of teachers whose power to control space, timetable and curriculum, together with the compulsory nature of schooling, may easily create an atmosphere of tension (Foster, 1990). The additional factors of teachers being predominantly middle class and white further complicate the nature of social control in multi-ethnic schools. Some students whom we interviewed indeed felt that teachers did sometimes try to engineer cross-ethnic mixing in lessons. On the whole, however, teachers who expressed a view did not feel it appropriate to try to manipulate student interactions in this way. We saw no evidence of teachers using their power to control inter-ethnic mixing directly or indirectly, as was found by Troyna (1978). However, we did hear of occasional *institutional* factors which might militate against students mixing together. For example, it was reported in one school that students on 'free dinners' had to queue in the hall; since most of these students were Bangladeshi it reinforced their separateness.

The dominant student group in most schools was obviously white. However, this group was no more homogeneous than the ethnic minority communities. There were sub-groupings based on class, gender and age. As was demonstrated in the discussion of student friendships, these factors often cut across ethnic and religious differences. We saw no evidence of white students using the power of numbers to exclude ethnic minority students from full integration. Where students were excluded it was because of factors which were just as likely to be used by ethnic minority students as white. As one student observed, when asked about whether white or black students were allowed to join in the informal soccer matches in the playground: 'It just depends who the ball belongs to'.

It would be easy to over-react to the tendency of some students in some schools to group by ethnicity. After all, most students in most schools spend their time in all-white groups. Small groups are constantly forming and reforming around friendships, social background, gender and common interests. In multi-ethnic schools, grouping on shared ethnic, linguistic or religious interests become that much more obvious. We agree in principle with the comment — already quoted above — of the teacher in a northern school:

> They do tend to stay in groups but it doesn't matter. We all find our own friends. Why should we force things?

We cannot, however, agree with those teachers who appeared to advocate a *general laissez-faire* response to that voluntary 'ethnic apartheid' among students which seemed to be an element in the life of two or three of the schools studied. Fortunately, while direct attempts to encourage mixing across ethnic groups as *such* run the risk of being clumsy and injudicious, the range of factors likely to be relevant to inter-ethnic relationships is wide; and most of them lie in areas of quite legitimate intervention by the school. Nevertheless, we acknowledge that it would be naive to deny that intra-ethnic grouping sometimes results from a sense of alienation or fear on the one hand, and aggressiveness and intimidation on the other. Schools need to be sensitive to the causes of grouping.

Responding to Abusive Behaviour

In Chapter 4 we introduced the central issue of inter-ethnic abuse — most commonly, name-calling, other forms of verbal abuse and bullying — through our general analysis of the perceived quality of inter-ethnic relationships in the schools. What was the extent of such behaviour and how did the schools respond to it?

Recent research has generated a considerable amount of data about that most ubiquitous aspect of student's inhumanity to student: verbal abuse, or name-calling (Akhtar and Stronach, 1986; Kelly, 1990; Wright, 1992). We also were interested in verbal abuse, for three reasons: because it might reflect the general atmosphere of inter-ethnic relationships in a school; because of the likely significance of a school's and teachers' response to the grosser forms of name-calling; and because of the possible connection between verbal and other, perhaps more serious, forms of abuse. Our investigation of name-calling made full use of quantitative (questionnaire) and qualitative (mainly interview) data.

The most commonly-reported *subject-matter* of verbal abuse across the nine schools, according to our questionnaire analysis, was race or colour, with nearly a quarter of students reporting being called names mentioning this. That is to be seen against the fact that well over half of the students said that they were 'not very often' called names they did not like; and that one-fifth reported that they were never called such names.

The second most commonly-mentioned criterion for name-calling was students' looks or physical features. While analysis by ethnic groups showed that ethnic minority students were much more likely than others to mention race/colour, religion and language as the subject-matter of experienced verbal abuse, white students most commonly mentioned looks or features. Although this is just what one would expect, it is noteworthy that verbal abuse which puts a person into a category, and abuses the category as well as the person, is likely to be doubly hurtful to the person. Membership of an ethnic and/or religious and/or linguistic minority therefore furnishes ample opportunities for that double hurt to be felt. Furthermore, we found through interviews that other categories than ethnicity surfaced, and were sometimes experienced as hurtful — for example, gender, class and wealth.

The frequency of reported (abusive) name-calling varied considerably between schools. Students in the schools with high proportions of one ethnic minority reported higher levels of name-calling on the whole than students in the more truly multi-ethnic schools. In the school reporting the highest level of verbal abuse, which was a largely 'bi-ethnic' school, only 3 per cent of ethnic minority students said that they were 'never' called names they disliked; 17 per cent of all the others said 'never'. A significantly higher proportion of Muslim students compared with others reported experiencing name-calling fairly or very often. Frequency also sometimes seemed to vary with age: in three of the schools, interviews suggested that there was less verbal abuse in the upper school. One of the three schools was strongly 'bi-ethnic' and reported one of the higher levels of name-calling overall. But in another, 'bi-ethnic', school, abuse was seen to be more common among year 10 than among year 8 students.

Students' reactions to name-calling were most tellingly revealed through interviews. The questionnaire analysis across all schools showed more than half of the students who experienced name-calling saying that it 'really doesn't bother me', with significantly higher proportions of ethnic minority students responding that it *did* bother them, and that they felt angry. However, interviews threw up a wide range of expressed feelings. It is striking that the deepest reported hurt was not always about abuse on 'racial' lines, but fairly often about insults to do with poverty, or class, or physical characteristics. Where ethnicity was the reported agenda for abuse, many students tended to say that they shrugged it off unless and until it became too persistent and vicious. On the other hand, ethnic minority students were more likely to feel angry about name-calling. Overall, we gained an impression of a high degree of patience — or, perhaps, resignation — among students who saw themselves as victims of name-calling. We also encountered a number of examples in interviews of white students expressing some interest and concern about apparently racist abuse of ethnic minority students, especially south Asians.

Some students we interviewed reported that their lives had at some point been made unhappy at school by racist taunts. However, interviews gave us the impression, strengthened by informal observation, that 'racial', ethnic and religious categories were used as weapons and reinforcers in the general context of student-student abusiveness, rather more than as the original *casus belli*. The fact that many students reported their own and others' use of 'racial' name-calling as means ('getting my own back') rather than ends, tends to underscore that impression. Whether or not the use of 'racial' categories in otherwise routine abusiveness escalates conflict to the point where it becomes serious confrontation is not a question about which our research enables us to generalise — even in the context of the nine schools studied. There was, however, some evidence that that was the case. Much, obviously, would depend on how schools, and in particular teachers, respond to such verbal abuse between students.

The extent to which teachers intervened in cases of verbal abuse both apparently varied between schools and was the subject of differing perceptions within schools. At one school, an Asian student who reported being a more or less regular victim of name-calling thought that 'teachers probably don't know it happens'. An Asian girl in the same school said that she did not experience name-calling because 'teachers tell people off if they call people names'. Yet another Asian student in that school said that 'teachers sorted it out.' In all schools some students said that teachers did little; some that teachers dealt with it effectively and some that they would rather deal with it themselves — either because of an 'anti-grassing' code, or because they feared retaliation from other students. It is interesting that, in the school for which the questionnaire data revealed the lowest level of 'racial' name-calling of all, older students reported in interviews that teachers had shown a willingness to intervene by dealing in exemplary fashion with 'racial' verbal abuse, and that the amount of such abuse had decreased. The contrast between that picture and other students' reports (even including one or two in the school just mentioned) of teachers' ignorance or indifference was striking.

Troyna (1991, *op. cit.*), it will be recalled, argues the necessity of

> teasing out the ideological lens through which children make sense of (the) world. . . .

That reminds us of the limitations and distorting effects of purely quantitative investigations of such phenomena as 'racial' name-calling. As with very many other factors relevant to inter-ethnic relationships, we were aware in our interviews with students about name-calling that their intended meanings would be likely to vary, and to be shaped by ideological, and therefore not wholly-conscious, assumptions. Conversely, however, we could not fail to be struck by the extent to which some students (even some second-years) exhibited sophistication and conscious reflection in their analysis of name-calling:

> Name-calling has more to do with the class factor. Racism has a lot to do with social class.

Joke-telling may, of course, be quite closely related to name-calling, in the sense that both may involve negative stereotypes. In the nine schools studied, ethnic minority students experienced more joke-telling based on race, religion or colour than did other students. Variations between ethnic minorities were interesting: Muslim students reported a higher level of joke-telling than ethnic/religious minorities in general. Three out of four Bangladeshi students reported that jokes were told about their 'race', religion or colour to some extent. Bangladeshi students were, of course, among the less well-established minorities (in terms of length of families' settlement in the UK) in the schools. As we have repeatedly seen in other contexts, there was a tendency for reported 'racial' joke-telling to be less frequent in the more ethnically diverse schools.

There was considerable variation between ethnic groups in responses to joke-telling of this kind. Responding to the questionnaire, Muslim students were much less likely to report that they found such jokes funny; ethnic minority students in general were more likely than others to say that they felt 'sad' or 'angry'. In interviews, most students' reactions were low-key; but some strongly negative reactions stood out — both from ethnic minority and from white students. Some white students expressed their strong disapproval of 'racial' jokes told about ethnic minorities; others mentioned jokes told about whites by Asians. Conversely, a Muslim girl at one school summarised very well the feelings of some minority students about the stereotyping inherent in much 'racial' joke-telling:

> We can't help it. We can't leave our religion. It makes me feel horrible. Sometimes I wished I shouldn't be a Muslim.

For the researchers, one of the most interesting findings about joke-telling was the incidence (not, admittedly, common) of reported jokes about black people told *by* black students. This was variously seen, by both white and black students, as acceptable, or as evidence of a crisis of identity. One is reminded here of Jewish humour (i.e. jokes told by Jews about themselves) which is almost invariably self-deprecating. Humour which mocks the foibles of one's own ethnic or national group may indeed be related to the problematics of ethnic identity; but it is as likely, perhaps, to reveal a certain confidence in that identity as it is to suggest insecurity. It depends very much upon whether 'own-group' jokes are essentially the same as the racist jokes told by others, or the sort of self-mocking humour which sees one's group as just an exemplar of human weaknesses in general. It is surely important for teachers as much as anyone else to be aware of the difference.

Perceptions of how teachers dealt with name-calling varied between students even in the same school. In all schools there were some students who said teachers did little, some who said teachers dealt with name-calling well and others who said that they would not tell teachers but would 'deal with it themselves' (often drawing on the help of friends or older siblings in school). Several students mentioned how school life had been made miserable by name-calling but that teachers had intervened and stopped it, for example, the Sikh student who reported that he had been called names because he wore a turban. 'It was caused by the poppadom advert on TV. My Mum came in and talked with the teachers and it was sorted out.'

However, other students were less likely to report name-calling to teachers, sometimes because the teachers were thought to be unconcerned, but more frequently because telling teachers was seen as unacceptable social behaviour within their peer group. There appeared to be a strong consciousness of the unacceptability amongst students interviewed of 'grassing'. As one student explained, 'I just ignore them. I don't want to cause trouble . . . I'd be called a grass' and another explained that 'no-one really grasses' in school. Fear of retaliation was also mentioned. A white girl who said she had been called 'racist' names added 'students do it just for fun, especially if you report it. They do it more then so you tend not to tell the teachers'. And another,

> I don't really tell them (teachers). It's just a waste of time. If you tell the teacher and they get told off they're just gonna do it more and call me a chicken or something.

The Swann Report (*op. cit.*) discussed the issue of name-calling and concluded that a distinction had to be made between general and racist name-calling.

> We believe that the essential difference between racist name-calling and other forms of name-calling is that whereas the latter may be related only to the individual characteristics of a child, the former is a reference not only to the child but also by extension to their family and indeed more broadly to their ethnic community as a whole.

Presumably, a similar point could be made about sexist name-calling which is also a slur on a wider group to which a person belongs. Certainly, name-calling related to gender was reported frequently by girls (although less so by boys). It must be said that in interviews, students did not make such fine distinctions. Indeed, the deepest hurt was often expressed by students who were called names on grounds to do with class or wealth (shown by where they lived or what clothes they wore) or a parent being 'called'.

In this sample, name-calling to do with race was reported most frequently, although among ethnic minority students, religion was also often mentioned. The responses of students towards name-calling of any kind was mixed, with many students saying in interview or indicating in the questionnaire that they tended to ignore it. More sophisticated students were able to talk about the significance or intent behind the words used. As Kelly (1990) suggests, based on her survey of selected Manchester schools, students are often more aware of the actual meanings and significance than teachers (not to mention researchers) looking in from the outside.

There is another important disciplinary issue associated with name-calling. Our evidence supports the view reported by Kelly and others that name-calling, even if it is not intended to be offensive, leads to a progressive breakdown in relationships between students resulting in increased inter-ethnic tension and hostility. Many students indicated on the questionnaire and explained in interviews that they called names in order to 'get their own back' and felt that other students did the same.

Research into bullying has been, until very recently, a neglected area in the United Kingdom (Tattum and Lane, 1989). A recent study examined the role of ethnicity in the experience of bullying with a sample of thirty-three pairs of Asian and white children (Moran, Smith, Thompson and Whitney, 1993). The results, based on individual interviews with children, showed that the most common forms of bullying were being called names (not about race), and being hit. It is interesting to note that only Asian children reported name-calling. It is difficult to draw clear lines between the sorts of verbal abuse typified by name-calling and racist jokes, and actual bullying. But we did treat bullying as a separate category of student experience, both in the questionnaire and — directly and indirectly — in interviews. Most students reported that they had never been bullied at school (60 per cent of girls and 54 per cent of boys). There was no significant difference in the pattern of reporting by ethnic minority students compared with all others. But there were significant differences *between* ethnic minorities: fewer Bangladeshis reported that they were never bullied than all others, and more said that it happened frequently. Interestingly, Afro-Caribbeans reported less experience of being bullied than all other students. Among the schools, two stood out: one ethnically very diverse school reported lower levels of bullying than most others schools, and a school with a strong concentration of one ethnic group reported higher levels. The differences were seen as statistically significant. The most common reason given by students for being bullied was 'because of my race or colour' (22 per cent). Ethnic minority students in general, and Bangladeshis in particular, although not reporting significantly higher levels of bullying than others, were much more likely than others to give 'race'/colour, religion or language as the cause of the bullying.

Interviews with students revealed considerable variety in their interpretations of 'bullying'. It seems that the word is as much part of the central terminology of school life as 'playground' or 'detention'. Thus, students often seemed disposed to use the word to refer to experiences much less serious than persistent harassment. Again, that argues caution in interpreting the quantitative evidence. However, we did hear disturbing reports by students, especially those from ethnic minority backgrounds and particularly (though not exclusively) Asians, of thoroughly nasty treatment by others. Examples included sexual harassment as well as bullying on ethnic criteria. These reports occasionally included mention of bullying between ethnic groups.

Altogether, in interviews students expressed a fair degree of confidence in teachers' willingness and ability to intervene in cases of bullying. Exceptions to this pattern presented themselves: in a school containing an absolute majority of Bengali students, teachers appeared to the researcher to be reluctant to confront persistent sexual harassment by Bengali boys of girls in the same ethnic group for fear of being seen as racist. There seemed to be some variety in students' degree of willingness to report cases of bullying to their teachers. One Bangladeshi student said that he did not tell teachers about bullying because he felt that their response was too soft. Some students complained about teacher indifference; others, about teachers' ignorance of what went on; still others, about the lack of a strong enough discipline structure in the school which would entail stronger action to deal with 'racial' abuse.

We have so far in this section on abuse summarised the variety of perceptions of name-calling, joke-telling and bullying in which there may have been a 'racial' dimension present. Some cases of inter-ethnic abuse may be characterised as 'racial' incidents — although what counts as a case thereof is notoriously difficult to define (see, for example, Waters, 1992). We suggest that a 'racial' incident is an episode or event in which there is conflict, abuse (which may be one-sided or mutual; physical and/or verbal) and the presence of supposed racial categories. That latter feature may be present in the ethnicities of those involved in the conflict; in the language used as weapons in the conflict; in the language used by the parties to the conflict in describing or explaining it; in any connections there may be between the conflict situation itself in a school and community divisions outside the school; or in any combination of those factors. As Zec (1993) has suggested, it is important that educators beware of re-describing that which they would prefer not to recognise. Thus, although some teachers may wish to locate certain kinds of name-calling merely within the general repertoire of what might be called student's inhumanity to student, they should always be prepared to listen to students' own descriptions of such behaviour. If, for example, a student sees him/herself as a victim of racism through verbal abuse, that perception should not be dismissed prematurely as evidence of a chip on the shoulder. On the other hand, in dealing with inter-ethnic abuse teachers and schools should explicitly treat it within a framework of equal opportunities and of general moral values, in which any denial of human worth, any negation of the principle of respect for persons, is to be called to account. In short, there should be a presumption in favour of treating as a 'racial' incident that which is seen as such by its actors; but any such event should also be treated as an affront to democratic values in general and therefore to the school.

How, then, did teachers and schools deal with 'racial' incidents? According to most students, these incidents were treated seriously. In only one school, however, did students think there was a written code of practice regarding racism — and even here they expressed uncertainty about its whereabouts. Nevertheless, in several schools written notices and posters were mentioned (and seen by the researchers) which transmitted anti-racist messages. Assembly was seen by some as an opportunity to warn students about racist behaviour. Other students stressed the existence of a 'student ethos' of anti-racism, which did more than the formal efforts of the school to combat racist behaviour. We have already seen (Chapter 3) that evidence from heads, staff and official documentation suggests that, although all schools had multi-cultural education and/or equal opportunities policy statements of some kind, formal rules and procedures for dealing with racist behaviour seemed only to exist in four or five of the schools (the uncertainty arises from the fact that we carried out research in the schools at times of change and development — highly fluid in some of them).

The question may well be asked whether a school which had a well-defined and published set of guidelines on dealing with 'racial' incidents was likely to deal with them more effectively than a school which did not. The variety of perception among staff between and within schools makes the question impossible to answer. Some elements of a systematic approach to 'racial' incidents certainly suggest themselves: unequivocal and public dedication by a school to the proposition that intolerance shall not be tolerated — to which the staff as a whole are seen to be committed; careful logging of 'racial' incidents by senior management, accompanied by reporting to the LEA (to whom or what would a grant maintained school report?); a real role for class and year teachers in dealing with incidents as they arise — this in order to reinforce the whole-school commitment to anti-racism; involvement of parents and, if necessary, local community representatives; and a determination to follow up a case after it has been defused, through educational and pastoral programmes — these are some of the desirable elements. We are not in a position to say that those schools where there appeared to be relatively systematic procedures were more serious and successful in dealing with incidents. Some headteachers and staff appeared genuine in their expressed view that dealing with 'racial' incidents in the context of normal disciplinary procedures was preferable to written codes; and we have already said that a school should make explicit the relationship between racist behaviour and *all* kinds of denial of human worth. In any case, some system such as has just been sketched out may well be seen in the context of a school's overall approach to discipline and social values. But — and this is crucial and reinforced by our experience of this research — no school, or headteacher, or teacher, should deceive themselves into believing that 'race' may be *subsumed under* school law and order in general, and thus lose its recognition as a most powerful factor in student-student conflict. We did come across examples of that tendency among teachers.

That last point needs to be balanced, however, by agreement with some teachers' emphasis on the need for a link between firm responses to racist behaviour and positive teaching about tolerance and acceptance. We also strongly agree with those teachers who stressed the importance of equality of treatment in dealing with incidents. Some white students across the nine schools expressed the view that they tended to be seen as the perpetrators, and black or Asian students as the victims, of abuse to an unfair extent. In one school some staff felt that black boys were dealt with too leniently. Whatever the truth of these matters (and it must be said that unconscious prejudice may have been a factor here), the potential link between those expressed feelings and the Burnage tragedy (see Macdonald, 1989) — where anti-racist policies pursued without sufficient sensitivity were seen as a causal factor — is obvious.

In those schools where systematic attempts appeared to be made to deal with 'racial' incidents, procedures varied but all involved some sort of documentary recording. More striking was the variety of perceptions even within schools as to what the recording procedure actually was, and whose responsibility it was. In at least one school staff opinion seemed to differ on whether the senior teacher who kept a log of incidents *should* do so, because of the contestability of the concept of racism. It is difficult to resist the judgment that there was more evidence of schools' seriousness about dealing with racism than there was of consistency, consensus and confidence within the schools in identifying and confronting it.

Teacher-Student Attitudes and Behaviour

The effective implementation of school policies (or principles) depends to some degree on the quality of inter-personal relationships — between the heads and their staff, between senior management and other teachers and by no means least, between teachers and students. It was not our intention to investigate teacher-student relationships. Students were not asked to comment on their teachers and the attitudes or competence of teachers was not discussed in staff interviews. However, inevitably perhaps, comments were made to us both by students and teachers about student-teacher relationships.

When students did speak about their teachers it was usually with approval or even affection. Sometimes it was teachers in general, as in the case of a year 8 girl in Fir School who said what she liked most about her school was that it had 'teachers who are actually human beings!' More often, it was one or two specific teachers who were held in high regard by students. Almost one in eight students (11.9 per cent) answering the questionnaire said that what they liked most about school was a specific teacher. Fewer students (6.7 per cent) mentioned teachers in general, the implication being that while many students value highly some teachers they are less than enthusiastic about teachers in general.

A similar pattern emerged from answers to questions about what students disliked most about school. A quarter of students (25.3 per cent) mentioned examples of specific teachers as something they particularly did not like about school (see the results for Q.25). Comments about teachers in general (7.6 per cent) were lower down the list after specific lessons (25.1 per cent), poor aspects of student relationships (17.1 per cent) and school rules (11.0 per cent), but before homework (7.0 per cent). However, these general patterns across the whole sample camouflage significant differences between schools. For example, in Larch School a much higher proportion of students (17.8 per cent) mentioned liking particular teachers and teachers in general (9.3 per cent) and disliking certain teachers (33.6 per cent) and teachers in general (8.4 per cent). In Oak School the proportion of students who said they liked certain teachers was much lower (7.0 per cent) with 20.1 per cent indicating that teachers in general were something they particularly disliked about school.

There were also differences in the patterns when analysed by ethnicity. In general, ethnic minority students were more likely than others to mention 'the teachers' as something they liked about school and less likely to mention teachers in general as something they disliked. However, ethnic minority students were less likely to identify a specific teacher as the object of particular approval or disapproval. These patterns were especially true for Bangladeshi students.

Although in interviews most students explained their dislike of specific teachers by reference to a single incident, others spoke of constantly being 'picked on'. There was often a feeling of injustice amongst such students. 'A couple of teachers just don't like my face.' 'I get picked on by teachers because I'm the biggest. I do mess around a bit, but I'm not the only one.' Associated with this was the perceived tendency of teachers to stereotype. A black year 10 student said: 'They continue to pick on you because you've done wrong in the past. They don't realise you can change.' Other students felt that they were hostages to the teachers' negative experiences of older siblings in school. Scapegoating by teachers and a tendency to use students to work out their frustrations were also mentioned. Several students said teachers picked on students who were not very clever. As a girl in Ash school put it, 'The less brainy ones are badly treated. Brainy students get more of the teachers' attention.' Another student observed, 'It's the ones with the brains that get the best treatment. Teachers need them to get the good marks.' An Anglo-Jewish girl said teachers always 'backed up each other' and they 'take their moods out on us'.

We also found evidence of ethnic minority students believing that their teachers had low expectations of them. For example, a black girl said she and her black friends were always given 'easy worksheets' to do by a particular teacher 'because of our appearance'. She explained, 'the teacher wouldn't say why we couldn't do the harder ones. I think it was because of racism'.

Occasionally, students, both black and white, argued that some of their teachers were 'racist'. Examples given by students to support this often suggested it was more likely to be ignorance, insensitivity or what Swann (*op. cit.*) called unconscious racism. White and Asian girls observed that quiet students, particularly Asian girls, who 'don't speak up' in lessons were not so well treated. In Pine School, a white girl commented that teachers did not pronounce Asian names properly and added 'we call them out until they get them right!'. But there were also suggestions from students that teachers knew what they were doing when they expressed racist attitudes. For example, the Asian boy who explained how some teachers addressed Asian students. 'If you are not eating properly, some teachers say to you "Why are you eating like a dog?" and they know that Muslims don't like dogs.'

In all but two of the schools comments were made by one or more teachers about the racist attitudes or behaviour of colleagues, from unhelpful to overtly racist. Such comments were relatively rare and often made reluctantly by teachers.

However, they included anti-semitic and 'anti-Muslim' remarks, racist jokes and laughing at students' names. In one school, a teacher felt that racist attitudes by some staff spoilt attempts to support ethnic minority students. 'You try to do things . . . to go out of your way to help Asian students. But some teachers go the other way. They make too many racist comments.' Another teacher in the same school observed, 'Some staff are definitely racist — and sexist. They express it in front of the students. Staffroom banter is a bit different. But they shouldn't say things in front of the students.' A teacher who felt the key to good relationships in school was to 'treat all students as human beings' added, 'there are some racist teachers — often those who can't respond to human beings of any colour!'. A probationary teacher at the end of the interview expressed concern at the 'overt racism' expressed by some staff. Although these were described as 'only the odd one or two', they did express their views openly in the staffroom. The teacher wondered if senior management who 'have their own territory and don't spend enough time in the staffroom' knew about it.

Occasionally, teachers recalled experiences of racist attitudes of students towards them. Most frequent was the concern expressed by female teachers about 'sexist attitudes' of older Muslim boys. In one southern school, four members of staff interviewed referred to students mimicking the accents of ethnic minority teachers. In the same school, a female Asian teacher recalled how on two occasions white and black boys had made fun of her by imitating a stereotypical Indian accent (although the teacher did not speak with an accent). This teacher did not feel that the incidents were of 'major significance' since, as she put it, '99 per cent of the kids . . . have never been directly racist to me'.

It was not the intention of the research to ask students about how they were treated by teachers or if teachers demonstrated racial prejudice. Indeed, we were surprised by the way in which students in some schools consistently interpreted a question which simply asked 'do you ever feel badly treated in school' in terms of treatment by teachers. However, students frequently had positive things to say about teachers during general discussions about experiences in school. Specific teachers were frequently mentioned by students in their response to the open question about what they liked most about school on the questionnaire. A smaller percentage of children interviewed were critical of specific teachers or teachers in general. Dislike of certain teachers was the most frequent response to the open question about what students liked least about school in the questionnaire.

Smith and Tomlinson (1989) found that although the child's enthusiasm for school is very little related to the level of praise received from teachers, it is fairly strongly (inversely) related to the level of blame. The evidence from this sample also indicates an overriding concern among some students about perceived mistreatment by teachers. For a few, this mistreatment included a racial element.

In the absence of any specific questions in the instruments it would be unwise to make generalisations about how students viewed the attitudes of teachers towards race or the responses of teachers to minority students. However, it was clear that a small proportion of students interviewed (both black and white) felt that some teachers were racially prejudiced in their treatment of ethnic minority students.

In most schools, this perception was supported by one or more of the teachers interviewed.

This chapter completes our analyses of factors relevant to inter-ethnic relationships, as they emerged from our study of nine schools. In the final chapter we shall try to distil from the complex data generated by our research a summary of main issues and findings, together with some practical implications suggested by this study for schools seeking to enhance the quality of inter-ethnic relationships among their students.

Chapter 7

Towards Good Inter-Ethnic Relationships

Preamble: Methodologies Revisited

As was made clear in Chapter 2, this research was prepared in an awareness of other relevant enquiries in this broad area which exemplify methodologies on the positivist-ethnographic continuum. Troyna (1991 *op. cit.*) has picked out 'two distinct methodologies' in empirical research in the area. Of the 'case study' approach taken by a number of enquiries into racial harassment in schools, he says:

> . . . (they) have collated an impressive range of evidence to demonstrate the tenacity and pervasiveness of 'racial' incidents in schools.

He contrasts that approach with

> . . . more formal, quantitative methods of analysing racial harassment. . . . A statistical profile of 'racial' incidents in schools has been built on pupil responses to questionnaires, word and sentence completion tests, structured classroom observation and interviews with students, parents and teachers. Interestingly, and in contrast to the general conclusions drawn from more discursive studies of this issue, quantitative researchers have been more circumspect about the prevalence of 'racial' incidents in schools.

Troyna acknowledges that 'anecdotal' evidence from case studies about 'racial' incidents in schools is often too imprecise and partial to be an adequate basis for generalisation, policy development and professional practice. But his critique of Kelly's (1990) study of racial name-calling in Manchester secondary schools, and of Smith and Tomlinson's (1989) *The School Effect* argues converse weaknesses in a 'supposedly more systematic 'approach. Both these studies report that overt racism is not on the whole a large-scale problem in multi-ethnic schools, or at any rate in those studied by them (three in Kelly's case, twenty in Smith and Tomlinson's). But the approach taken by these researchers is, Troyna believes, open to three main criticisms: first, that the apparent absence of 'overt racism' does not necessarily negate claims about the prevalence or seriousness of racist behaviour; second, that in relying on others', especially parents', perceptions of children's experiences in school, rather than on students' reports of their own experiences couched in their own language, such enquiries are likely to miss the 'subtle and complex nature of racism in education' through failing to register the narrative of the main actors; third that studies of the Smith and Tomlinson type tend to concentrate on 'assembling statistical data on the observable, detectable and therefore easily measurable forms of racism.' As such, they may be influential in areas of policy and programmes of action; but may also 'sacrifice understanding . . . on the altar of description.'

In deciding at the start to employ a 'mixed-method' research approach, embodied in multi-site case studies, we were aiming essentially to do three things: first, penetrating school students' and teachers' experience of inter-ethnic relationships through recording what they would tell; second, implementing that procedure across nine very roughly similar institutions, with the anticipated (and realised) outcomes of both illuminating variety and some suggestive patterning; third, exploiting the number of institutional case studies to carry out a quantitative analysis based on a large (2,300) student sample.

The result, not surprisingly, has been the generation of a very large amount of ethnographic data, against a substantial backdrop of statistical material. The latter, however, is not entirely of the sort criticised for its limitations by Troyna: the questionnaire (see below, Appendix 3) was administered exclusively to the whole year 8 and year 10 student cohorts from which the interviewees were taken; and its questions followed closely the subject-matter of the interview schedules (see below, Appendix 2) but without, on the whole, offering opportunities for discursive response. There is, therefore, a relationship between the qualitative and quantitative data, and that this is so is borne out in the main body of this book (see, for example, Chapters 3 and 4). It is readily acknowledged that that relationship could well be further explored. It is also clear that the size of the questionnaire sample, and the very large number of possible variables and combinations of variables embedded in it, called for a lot more analysis than the time and resources available to this study were able to yield. (It was indeed possible to undertake *some* analysis which went beyond crude whole-sample frequency and which yielded some striking information: see, for example, Chapter 4, Table 4.3).

Furthermore, earlier chapters illustrate just that difference in texture between quantitative and qualitative research to which Troyna refers in his critique. We are convinced that, although this study has proved more complex than would have been the case had either approach been used on its own, the interaction between the two has been fruitful.

Common Issues and Salient Findings

Issues are treated here as 'common' in the sense that in our judgment they were issues for, and arose in, all of the schools used in this study; further, that they are likely to be issues for secondary schools and teachers in general. The 'salient findings', on the other hand, did not necessarily emerge in all the nine schools. The criterion for highlighting particular findings in the body of this book has throughout been suggestiveness rather than ubiquity.

The material which formed the basis for Chapters 3 to 6 of this book enables us in this final chapter to group a summary of findings into seven interrelated issues, each seen as influencing, or constitutive of, inter-ethnic relationships, as follows:

- inter-cultural knowledge and understanding between students, and of students by teachers (Chapters 3 and 5);
- the influence of LEA and school policies (Chapter 3);
- the relevance of curricular and cross-curricular activities (Chapter 5);
- the role of extra-curricular activities (Chapter 5);
- the nature and extent of mixing between students of different ethnicities, and factors which appeared to influence it (Chapters 4 to 6);
- the nature, extent and determinants of various kinds of abuse between students of different ethnicities; and schools' responses to abuse (Chapters 4 and 6);
- aspects of teachers' attitudes and behaviour towards students of ethnic minority origin — including students' perceptions of 'racism' in teachers (Chapters 4 and 6).

In addition, some overall summary points are made below about the quality of inter-ethnic relationships in the research schools, as perceived by students, teachers and the researchers (Chapter 4).

Inter-Cultural Knowledge and Understanding

- Students and teachers seemed to agree that what students from different groups knew about each other's cultures arose more from life than from planned school provision. Perhaps not surprisingly, more ethnic (and/or religious) minority students than all other students claimed to know 'quite a bit' or 'a lot' about each other's cultures; and four times as many Muslim students as all others.

- Variations between schools in the reported extent of inter-cultural knowledge did not seem to correlate well with differences in the perceived quality of inter-ethnic relationships between the schools. Yet teachers in all of the schools tended to be intuitively convinced of the importance of such knowledge to good relationships. Our impression was that, on the whole, levels of inter-cultural knowledge in the schools were too low to permit a definite conclusion to be drawn about the likely effect of high levels of such knowledge; however, some specific examples of effective promotion of what might be called 'cognitive interaction' between cultures did suggest that much might be achieved from such efforts.

- Teachers tended to confess relative ignorance of students' cultural backgrounds whatever the proportion of ethnic minority students was in each of the schools studied — and the schools did not know enough about the demographic profiles of their student intakes. Relatively few teachers were sufficiently prepared, through professional development activity, to work with maximum effectiveness in the multi-ethnic setting.

- The schools either did not have significant numbers of ethnic minority teachers, or revealed shortcomings in the way they treated them.

The Influence of LEA and School Policies

- Virtually all teachers were aware that their LEA had a policy on equal opportunities and anti-racist/multi-cultural education, but many felt uncertain about what was in it. Many teachers criticised LEA policies for their lack of suggested strategies for implementation, and for being platitudinous and superficial. Others criticised them for being overstated and possibly alienating.

- School policies on equal opportunities and anti-racist/multi-cultural education differed markedly between the nine schools studied, in terms of: stage of development; degree of formality and specificity, and the process of policy formulation. The most common approach to policy formulation was through a working group. In some cases, this approach exemplified a 'whole-school' process in policy formulation generally, with the aim of ensuring the widest possible ownership of policy. In others, working groups were perceived in precisely the opposite way: as a marginal activity conducted by 'enthusiasts'. Schools differed in the extent to which policy formulation in this area was given legitimacy and status by, for example, the direct participation of the headteacher or other senior management personnel in the process.

- There was little evidence of careful reflection by the participants or by senior management on the nature of the group process in the context of policy formulation by working group.

- At one school in which the school's policy on 'racist' abuse was discussed with students in tutorial groups, there was a lower level of reported name-calling on the basis of 'race' or colour of skin than at all the other schools studied. It is unnecessary to claim a causal nexus in order to find such a correlation suggestive. At another school, students were involved in the implementation and development of equal opportunities policy, to the extent of drafting public documentation together with the headteacher.

- At all the schools studied, teachers' perceptions of the value and effectiveness of school policies in this area varied widely, from unqualified enthusiasm, to critical support, to impatience with limitations, to cynicism. A small minority of teachers were opposed to any policy — formal or informal — on principle. It seemed to us, on the basis of interviews with teachers and, to a lesser extent, with students, that the perceived effectiveness and value of policies turned on questions of ownership, implementation and monitoring. The latter, in particular, was not strongly evident as developed practice in any of the schools studied.

- The schools which subsumed policy on racism and related matters under a general disciplinary framework of mutually respectful behaviour, and had no formal policy on racism etc. *as such*, did not 'come off worst' in respect of perceived quality of inter-ethnic relationships.

- The impact of central government policies on the status and viability of LEAs and their educational services makes the influence of LEA policies on equal opportunities and related subjects problematic.

The Relevance of Curricular and Cross-Curricular Provision

- Teachers' own preparedness to implement a curriculum for cultural diversity was limited, in particular in the light of the relative paucity of systematic and relevant professional development encountered among teachers in the nine schools used in this study. On the other hand, there was a near-unanimous feeling expressed by those teachers interviewed that the curriculum should be expected to play a role in developing students' inter-cultural knowledge and understanding. Variations in potential between subjects were predictably wide, with arts and humanities subjects being seen as the most effective vehicles. Some senior managements were seen as the driving force behind curriculum and related initiatives. Others were seen as being more interested in containing conflict than in backing creative change. There were wide differences of perception within as well as between school staffs here. The more ethnically diverse the student and teacher populations in the schools were, the more polarised views were among the staff about the extent of official support for curriculum and other change in this area.

- From examples of anti-racist/multi-cultural curriculum delivery encountered in this study, and from interviews with teachers, it was evident that, for some teachers, teaching/learning strategies, styles of delivery and 'codes of classroom practice' mattered more than curriculum content. Students seemed to remember examples of process-oriented classroom experiences designed to foster better relationships, such as group work, PSE activities in tutorial periods and the like, more than specific curriculum content 'on other' cultures — although religious education did throw up some examples, acknowledged by students, of inter-cultural learning which was perceived as useful.

- We were made aware of determined and sustained efforts of teachers to involve certain minority groups in curriculum activities which were seen as beneficial for relationships, even where responses by students and parents were sometimes unfavourable because of infringement of cultural/religious taboos. But most students seemed not to be conscious of curricular aims of imparting world perspectives or awareness of cultural diversity in Britain.

- The extent to which development of knowledge and values appropriate to good inter-ethnic relationships was addressed across the faculties and departments of the schools, reflected the extent to which there was a whole-school approach to relationships. In some of the nine schools studied there seemed to be a high level of consciousness of the importance of inter-ethnic relationships, and this was reflected across the curriculum. In others, the picture was much more fragmented, and curriculum responses to ethnic diversity were relatively dependent on individual initiative.

- Recent government legislation on the curriculum has called into question the extent to which real curriculum opportunities in the areas of equal opportunities and cultural diversity continue to exist.

The Role of Extra-Curricular Activities

- The prevailing view among teachers was that involvement by ethnic minorities in extra-curricular activities entailed informal contact with other students and with staff, and thus promoted good inter-ethnic relationships. However, although some ethnic minority groups were reasonably well-represented in some activities, Muslim students, and particularly girls, were consistently under-represented. In sport, the non-participation of Asian students in general, and Muslims in particular, was noticeable. Examples were also encountered of apparent insensitivity to ethnic minority students' cultural identities in the choice of plays for performance.

- Evidence presented by most teachers indicated that the number and scope of extra-curricular activities was in decline.

Inter-Ethnic Mixing

- Students tended to report that they were more likely to be in the company of friends from their own ethnic background in their neighbourhood, than in school. In the sample of schools studied, the more multi-ethnic the school, the more students tended to report that they drew their 'close friends' from ethnic groups other than their own. Patterns of stronger intra-ethnic preference emerged in the schools where there was bipolar ethnicity, in particular where there were sizeable Muslim groups.

- In the 'bi-ethnic' schools, even where students reported that relationships were not bad, students in interviews tended implicitly to adopt a 'negative' model of good relationships — in which 'keeping self to self' was seen as evidence of a satisfactory situation. Teachers in schools where intra-, rather than cross-ethnic mixing was the dominant pattern, often justified it on the grounds that it was wrong to force artificial interaction, and that 'pride in heritage' was to be encouraged. Many teachers, however, both at those schools and at others where cross-ethnic mixing was common, did feel that interaction between groups was important for good inter-ethnic relationships in the schools as a whole; and that the growth of large, monolithic groups of students from a particular ethnic minority background, sometimes in a numerical majority in the school, was bad for relationships in the school as a whole.

- In the more ethnically diverse schools, Afro-Caribbean students were the most likely minority to group together. This was sometimes seen as threatening by both other students and teachers. On the whole, however, teachers saw cross-ethnic grouping in the classroom as more to be encouraged — and as more common — than in non-formal situations. Once again, however, bipolarity in the classroom was to be seen more commonly in the 'bi-ethnic' than in the more truly multi-ethnic schools. Teachers were not sympathetic to the idea of making students sit in ethnically mixed groups.

- No evidence was seen of white students using the power of numbers to exclude ethnic minority students. Inclusions and exclusions arose from factors which often cut across ethnic and religious differences.

Inter-Ethnic Abuse and Schools' Responses to It

- The most commonly-reported subject-matter of verbal abuse across the nine schools studied, according to the questionnaire administered to all year 8 and 10 students, was race or colour. Analysis by ethnic groups showed that ethnic minority students were much more likely than others to mention race/colour, language or religion as the subject-matter of experienced verbal abuse. Students in the schools with high proportions of one ethnic minority reported higher levels of name-calling than students in the more truly multi-ethnic schools, and a significantly higher proportion of Muslim students than others reported experiencing name-calling fairly or very often.

- Interviews suggested that, although more ethnic minority students than others reported that name-calling bothered them and made them angry, many said that they shrugged it off unless it became too vicious and persistent. Interviews also yielded the impression to the researchers that 'racial', ethnic and religious categories were used as weapons and reinforcers in the general context of student-student abusiveness, rather more than as the central theme.

- There was wide variation in students' perceptions of how far teachers were prepared to intervene in cases of verbal abuse. In the school for which the questionnaire data revealed the lowest level of 'racial' name-calling of all, it was reported that teachers had intervened in exemplary fashion in such cases, and that the amount of such abuse had decreased. There was, however, much evidence of reluctance to report verbal abuse to teachers, either because the latter were seen as indifferent; or because of an anti-grassing code; or because of fear of retaliation.

- Students, in talking about bullying in interviews, seemed to use the word in at least two different ways: while some did mean persistent and sometimes physically violent harassment, others equated 'bullying' with occasional general abuse. There were, however, disturbing reports by students of what can only be described as serious bullying with a strongly 'racial' flavour. Such reports came mainly from students from ethnic minority backgrounds. On the whole, in interviews students expressed a fair degree of confidence in teachers' willingness and ability to intervene in cases of bullying. On the other hand, some students complained about teacher indifference; others, about teachers' ignorance of what was going on; still others, about the lack of a strong enough discipline structure in the school to ensure tough action to deal with bullying.

- About half of the schools studied had formal rules or procedures for dealing with apparently racist behaviour. There was great variety of perception among staff about whether a school which had a well-defined and published set of guidelines on dealing with 'racial' incidents was more likely to deal with them effectively than a school which did not.

- Some teachers showed reluctance to see 'racial' abuse — verbal or physical — as separate in any way from the issue of school law and order in general; they thus were not prepared to recognise it as a powerful factor in student-student conflict. We do not accept that view. We do agree, however, with some teachers' emphasis on the need for a link between firm responses to racist behaviour and positive teaching about tolerance, acceptance and respect for persons. We also acknowledge the careful formulation by some of the schools studied of a stance on racist behaviour which contextualises it within a general framework of commitment to democratic values.

- Some teachers interviewed stressed the importance of equality of treatment in dealing with 'racial' incidents. Some staff and students felt that white students were too readily seen as the perpetrators. We felt that, in some of these cases, unconscious prejudice was dictating the perception; but the importance of the issue — particularly in the light of cases such as the Burnage tragedy — cannot be overstated.

- Across the nine schools, there was more evidence of seriousness about dealing with racism than there was of consistency, consensus and confidence within the schools in identifying and confronting it.

Teachers' Attitudes and Behaviour

- Although the research yielded a fair number of examples of reports by students of 'bad treatment' by teachers, with ethnic minority students sometimes, and white students occasionally, citing 'racism' as a teacher's motive, the balance of evidence was in no way conclusive. Of those students referring to teachers' 'racism', Asians were disproportionately the source of such reports. Some ethnic minority students reported experiences of low expectations and stereotyping by teachers.

- A large number of students from a variety of backgrounds saw bad behaviour by students as having as much to do with general teacher-student conflict as teachers' attitudes. There were, however, many cases brought to our attention of students alleging being 'picked on' by individual teachers. It was difficult to discern a pattern here which related to the focus of this research; but Chapter 6 provides suggestive illustrations of the perceived nature and grounds of these confrontations.

- Some ethnic minority students also said, quite directly, that some of their teachers were 'racist'. We gained the impression from the way in which students reported this that these were mainly cases of unconscious racial prejudice, rather than of intentional discrimination of abuse. Students' reported experiences were, however, accompanied by similar perceived cases encountered by us in interviews with teachers and in less formal staffroom conversations. They were a case for concern.

- Some teachers reported examples of racism among their colleagues. Such reports referred to conscious and overtly expressed behaviour in the classroom and staffroom, rather than only to 'unconscious' stereotyping and the like. As reported to us, the cases were relatively few in number, but clearly worrying — even agonizing — to those reporting them. For us, they were a cause for concern out of proportion to their frequency.

The Quality of Inter-Ethnic Relationships

- Most students whose views were sought in questionnaire and interview, and most teachers interviewed, in all of the schools, felt that the quality of inter-ethnic relationships was quite good or better. Questionnaire and interview evidence, which were on the whole well-aligned, suggested that ethnic minority students had a less positive view of the state of inter-ethnic relationships in their schools than others; that this was particularly true of Bangladeshi students (and of others from newly- or recently-arrived families such as refugees); that students of Afro-Caribbean origin felt if anything more positively than students in general; that this feeling was sometimes unreciprocated, and that membership of a religious minority *as such* did not materially affect the picture.

- Some headteachers and their colleagues tended to define 'good inter-ethnic relationships' as 'absence of overt conflict'; others, more positively as, for example 'high levels of social interaction between groups'. The more ethnically diverse the school, the higher the level of expectation revealed in definitions appeared to be. Furthermore, the weight of quantitative data and qualitative evidence strongly suggested that, the more multi-ethnic a school was, the better its student-student relationships were felt to be. That conclusion arises from consideration of indirect evidence (for example on degrees of cross-ethnic mixing; inter-ethnic abuse) as well as from responses from students and teachers directly on the issue of relationships.

• Some schools were more powerful than others in fashioning their own destinies and managing their internal and external relationships (for examples, student recruitment; breadth of catchment area; stability of staff establishment). Not surprisingly, the perceived state of inter-ethnic relationships was better in the more 'powerful' schools. There also seemed to be a correlation between the quality of inter-ethnic relationships and the extent to which senior management were able and prepared to set a strong, positive and active tone. On the other hand, there appeared to be an association between the quality of inter-ethnic relationships and the degree to which staff as a whole were actively and persistently engaged in monitoring them.

• In schools where there was little or no ethnic minority representation on the teaching staff, and where reported levels of inter-cultural knowledge and understanding were among the lowest of the nine schools studied, the perceived quality of inter-ethnic relationships appeared to be relatively poor. But the presence of ethnic minority staff in itself was not necessarily correlated with good relationships. Ethnic minority teachers' contractual position, the extent to which they were marginalised by the reason for being on the staff, and their general treatment as colleagues — these were issues which seemed to correlate with how good a school's inter-ethnic relationships were.

Implications

The following implications for schools seem to us to stem directly from our findings.

• A school should seek to get to know its students very well. This is clearly a goal for all schools. However, the more complex the community of the school the more important it is that the broad characteristics of the various ethnic and religious groups represented are understood. This understanding, however, must go beyond these generalised characteristics to the complex patterns of cultural development and religious practices *within* specific communities. Ethnic monitoring and profiling are beginning to be used effectively by some schools to build up a clearer picture of broad patterns of ethnicity in school and to draw on this in ensuring equality of opportunity and appropriate provision for all students. But to know, for example, that 35 per cent of students are drawn from Afro-Caribbean backgrounds does not necessarily help teachers to appreciate the particular circumstances of any individual black student in relation to his or her experience of racism, acculturation or family background.

- This study has demonstrated that many teachers are creatively engaged in responding to cultural diversity. They are often open to new cultural experiences and are sensitive to ethnic minority needs. We were struck by the fact that where such qualities were present they were more to do with the personality and personal biography of individual teachers than the quality of their professional training and development. For such teachers there is much that can be built on in providing a deeper understanding of the specific ethnicity of their students and the relevance of this to their teaching. There are other teachers, of course, who are equally lacking in specific professional training in aspects of pluralism but who do not have the wider life experiences (or sometimes even the inclination) to respond to cultural diversity in school. Schools should therefore be concerned that its teachers become inter-culturally literate, at least to some extent and in some areas; this will have clear implications for professional development programmes and, in the content of devolved budgets and scarce resources, opportunities should be seized where possible to use resources exemplified by staff and others in the schools.

  Of course, just as 'add on' approaches to the curriculum are not the most effective way of countering ethnocentric teaching, so extra INSET sessions on aspects of cultural diversity may not be the most effective way of equipping teachers to understand their students better. The more such matters *permeate* all INSET programmes, the less demanding they become on scarce resources and the more directly relevant they will be seen to be by teachers. We believe that departments or faculties should include in their policy statements and development plans a commitment to ensuring that all teachers are growing in their understanding of the diverse backgrounds of their students. They should also address the implications this might have for teaching programmes and strategies. That is one way of encouraging permeation and of avoiding the temptation to devolve such matters to support staff or particular multi-cultural 'enthusiasts'.

- Schools should be tireless and constant in their determination to inform, consult, explain and persuade in implementing policy and practice in the areas of inter-ethnic relationships and equality of opportunity in general. Unless all groups in a school feel that what it is trying to do belongs to them, and that they share the responsibility for what goes on, the atmosphere of inter-ethnic relationships may be superficially satisfactory, but it is unlikely that good relationships, seen in the richer sense advocated in this study, will take root. Genuine equality of opportunity will not be achieved by mere compliance with the relevant legislation. It can be achieved only if those concerned have the *will* to formulate equal opportunities that are fully implemented, carefully monitored and reviewed.

- Schools should seek to recruit, retain and promote minority teachers. That need not entail positive discrimination of the sort that would be illegal; it *would* entail a legally and morally legitimate policy of affirmative action. Ethnic minority teachers should never be marginalised, whatever the official reason for their appointment. Some schools in this study were more successful than others in achieving this. Where schools were unsuccessful in recruiting minority teachers it was not necessarily an indication of lack of commitment or effort. National statistics indicate that ethnic minority students are not equally represented in initial teacher training courses. In general, there is a shortage of ethnic minority teachers and, from some groups (for example, the Afro-Caribbean community), representation is particularly low. The needs of individual schools cannot be understood outside the wider context of recruitment to teaching. We welcome recent initiatives by the DFE agency Teacher as a Career (TASC) and some training institutions to increase recruitment to teaching from minority communities, though we would not want to associate ourselves with the kind of institutional racism which assumes that ethnic minority teachers should be recruited only for multi-ethnic schools — all children need to experience the qualities that teachers from ethnic minorities can bring to schools. Where headteachers and governors have been successful in recruiting teachers from ethnic minority backgrounds it has often been as a result of a combination of strategies, including advertising in the ethnic minority press, statements welcoming applications from black teachers and personal contacts.

- The advent of the National Curriculum may have reduced the freedom on the part of schools to determine the content of lessons but assumptions remain unchanged as to their duty to inculcate standards of behaviour based on justice and mutual respect. Of course, such lessons are learnt not only through formal teaching but also implicitly in the way schools are organised and conduct their affairs, and explicitly in the policies and priorities which each school adopts. A school and its curriculum managers should be clear that, (even) within the National Curriculum, the opportunities for routinising a multi-cultural curriculum, in all subjects, *on good educational grounds*, are plentiful (see, for example, Pumfrey and Verma, 1993). That should be a priority. There is no excuse — or need — for an ethnocentric curriculum. But that does not mean a trivial differentiation purely on the basis of 'cultural' content and according only to the ethnic groups which happen to be present in the school. Inter-cultural knowledge alone cannot, of course, determine the quality of inter-ethnic relationships; community factors influence the quality of inter-ethnic life in school. As in the case of developing teachers' general understanding of their students, we believe that the permeating of curriculum INSET programmes with more international perspectives is the most likely way of achieving this.

- A school should seek to maximise the opportunities available for extra-curricular activities, especially those in which ethnic minority students can realistically participate.

- A school mainly containing a polarity of two ethnic groups — say, white Anglo-Saxon and Bengali — should do all it can to prevent that polarity turning into *polarisation*. That is easier said than done; but it is better to try without complete success to bring groups together than to accept and then rationalise an informal apartheid.

- Schools should build a clear, democratically formulated and pervasive framework of democratic values, and should locate their determination to confront the repertoire of inter-ethnic abuse within that framework. Senior managers should consistently manifest their commitment to it. Whether or not that code of values takes the form of a written constitution is, perhaps, less important. But the code should be accompanied by clear procedures which involve class and year teachers, parents and the community, and which are publicly known. The contexts for inter-ethnic conflict are so often those situations in which hostile, derogatory, hurtful, insulting and generally negative remarks or jokes are made to and about persons. A written agreed statement outlawing such behaviour, ratified by the governing body and included in the school's equal opportunities policy, is in our view a necessity. The fact that the behaviour will not thereby be extinguished is not a good reason for failure on the part of the school to repudiate it.

- A school should not hesitate to repudiate any tendency of members of its staff (academic, administrative or ancillary) to manifest racist attitudes or behaviour. A culture of prejudice or stereotyping among staff should be unequivocally rejected.

- Schools must acknowledge and accept that racist attacks and racism do not begin and end at the school gates but are part and parcel of a wider society within which schools play a role.

- School governors have the responsibility under the law to make sure that there is no negative discrimination of any type taking place; they are in a good position to influence change. Governors, by working with the headteacher, staff, parents and local authority, should aim to provide the best learning environment. Racism in any form hinders learning and tackling it should be seen as a matter of urgent priority.

Epilogue

In this study we have throughout been aware of Basil Bernstein's aphorism 'Schools cannot compensate for Society'. In recent years some research studies have suggested that schools do, in fact, make a difference. This study has been based on that latter premise, without ignoring Bernstein's wisdom. The data it has yielded has entirely persuaded us of the importance of good inter-ethnic relationships in a school. This is no peripheral matter, such that good relationships are just a bonus, or bad ones just an irritant, compared with the 'real' business of effective curriculum delivery, getting good examination results and achieving high enrolment levels. Good relationships are inseparable from all those other imperatives. Bad, or threadbare, inter-ethnic relationships entail a waste of opportunities and that lowering of academic standard which must, it is contended, stem from poor social relations. No attempt has been made in this study to demonstrate causal connections between the state of relationships and, for example, student attainment; it is not at all clear how that could be done. What has been demonstrated, it is hoped, is the centrality of inter-ethnic relationships to all aspects of the life of a multi-ethnic school and, conversely, the relevance of all the main elements of the institutional life of the school to its inter-ethnic relationships.

A Bengali boy in one of the research schools shall have (nearly) the last word:

> Sometimes you might see a white girl going out with a black boy and I've got black friends in my class and I find them funny and good friends. They say things and make me laugh. I think they're all right to be with.

There is, perhaps, some encouragement in reflecting that, across nine inner-city multi-ethnic schools, that comment was by no means untypical. We suggest that, for *any* multi-ethnic school to strive to make a comment of that sort unremarkable, would be an aim worth embracing.

Bibliography

ADELMAN, C. and YOUNG, M.F.D. (1985) 'The assumptions of educational research: The last twenty years in Great Britain', in SHIPMAN, M. (Ed) *Educational Research: Principles, Polices and Practices*, Lewes, The Falmer Press.

AKHTAR, S. and STRONACH, I. (1986) 'They call me blacky', *Times Educational Supplement*, 19.9.86.

ALEXANDER, Z. and DEWJEE, A. (1984) *Wonderful Adventures of Mrs Seacole in Many Lands*, Bristol, Falling Wall Press.

ANWAR, M. (1979) *The Myth of Return: A Study of Pakistanis in Britain*, London, Heinemann Educational Books.

ANWAR, M. (1988) 'Muslims, community and the issues in education', in O'KEEFFE, B. (Ed) *Faith, Culture and the Dual System: A Comparative Study of Church and County Schools*, Lewes, The Falmer Press.

ATKINSON, P. and DELAMONT, S. (1985) 'Bread and dreams or bread and circuses? A critique of case study research in education', in SHIPMAN, M. (Ed) *Educational Research: Principles, Polices and Practices*, Lewes, The Falmer Press.

BAGLEY, C. (1972) 'Patterns of inter-ethnic marriage in Britain', *Phylon*, **33**.

BALL, W. and TROYNA, B. (1987) 'Resistance, rights and rituals: denominational schools and multi-cultural education', *Journal of Education Policy*, **2**, 1.

BERRY, J. (1979) 'Research in Multi-cultural Societies: Implications of cross-cultural methods', *Journal of Cross-Cultural Psychology*, **10**, pp. 415–34.

BOLTON, E. (1979) 'Education in a multi-racial society', *Trends in Education*, Winter 1979, London, HMSO.

BULLIVANT, B. (1980) 'Searching for an ideology of pluralism', *Ethnic and Racial Studies*, **3**, October 1980.

BULLIVANT, B. (1984) *Pluralism: Cultural Maintenance and Evolution*, Clevedon, England, Multilingual Matters.

BULLIVANT, B. (1987) *The Ethnic Encounter in the Secondary School*, Lewes, The Falmer Press.

CARROLL, B. and HOLLINSHEAD, G. (1993) 'Ethnicity and conflict in physical education', *British Educational Research Journal*, **19**, 1.

CARTER, D.E. *et al.* (1980) 'Interracial acceptance in the classroom', in FOOT, H.C. (Ed) *Friendship and Social Relations in Children*, Chichester, John Wiley and Sons.

CASHMORE, E.E. (1984) *Dictionary of Race and Ethnic Relations*, London, Routledge and Kegan Paul.

CHAZAN, B. (1980) 'Models of ethnic education: The case of Jewish education in Britain', *British Journal of Educational Studies*, **26**, 1.

CLARK, N. (1992) 'Dachwyng Saturday School', in OHIC, A., MANNING, B. and CURNO, P. (Eds) *Community Work and Racism*, London, Routledge and Kegan Paul.

COHEN, L. and MANION, L. (1983) *Multi-cultural Classrooms — Perspectives for Teachers*, London, Croom Helm.

COHEN, L. and MANION, L. (1989) *Research Methods in Education*, London, Routledge and Kegan Paul.

COMMISSION FOR RACIAL EQUALITY (1985) *Review of the Race Relations Act: Proposals for Change*, London, Commission for Racial Equality.

COMMISSION FOR RACIAL EQUALITY (1987) *Racial Attacks: A Survey in Eight Areas of Britain*, London, Commission for Racial Equality.

COMMISSION FOR RACIAL EQUALITY (1988) *Learning in Terror*, London, Commission for Racial Equality.

COMMISSION FOR RACIAL EQUALITY (1990) *Britain: A Plural Society*, London, Commission for Racial Equality.

COMMISSION FOR RACIAL EQUALITY (1992) *Second Review of the Race Relations Act 1976*, London, Commission for Racial Equality.

CORNFORD, J. (1985) 'Annex G: A Note on Research', in DES, *Education for All, The Report of the Committee of Inquiry into the Education of Children from Ethnic Minority Groups* (The Swann Report), London, HMSO.

CRAFT, M. (Ed) (1984) *Education and Cultural Pluralism*, Lewes, The Falmer Press.

CROLL, C. (1986) *Systematic Classroom Observation*, Lewes, The Falmer Press.

DEAKIN, N. (1970) *Colour, Citizenship and British Society*, London, Panther.

DENZIN, N. (1970) *The Research Act*, Chicago, Aldine.

DEPARTMENT OF EDUCATION AND SCIENCE (DES) (1965) *Circular 7/65*, London, HMSO.

DEPARTMENT OF EDUCATION AND SCIENCE (DES) (1971) *The Education of Immigrants*, Educational Survey 13, London, HMSO.

DEPARTMENT OF EDUCATION AND SCIENCE (DES) (1974) *Educational Disadvantage and the Educational Needs of Immigrants*, London, HMSO.

DEPARTMENT OF EDUCATION AND SCIENCE (DES) (1981) *West Indian Children in Our Schools: Interim Report of the Committee of Inquiry into the Education of Children from Ethnic Minority Groups* (The Rampton Report), London, HMSO.

DEPARTMENT OF EDUCATION AND SCIENCE (DES) (1985) *Education for All, The Report of the Committee of Inquiry into the Education of Children from Ethnic Minority Groups* (The Swann Report), London, HMSO.

DOCKREL, W.B. (1980a) 'The contribution of research to knowledge and practice', in DOCKREL, W.B. and HAMILTON, D. (Eds) *Rethinking Educational Research*, London, Hodder and Stoughton.

DUNCAN, C. (1987) in CHIVERS, T.S. (Ed) *Race, Culture and Education*, London, Nelson.

DUMMETT, A. (1984) *A Portrait of English Racism*, London, Caraf Publications Ltd.

FILE, N. and POWER, C. (1981) *Black Settlers in Britain 1555–1958*, London, Heinemann.

FOSTER, P. (1990) *Policy and Practice in Multi-cultural and Anti-racist Education*, London, Routledge and Kegan Paul.

GALTON *et al.* (1980) *Inside the Primary Classroom*, London, Routledge and Kegan Paul.

GILLBORN, D. (1990) *Race, Ethnicity and Education: Teaching and Learning in Mult-ethnic Schools*, London, Routledge.

GILLBORN, D. and DREW, D. (1992) 'Race, class and school effects', *New Community*, **18**, 4, July 1992.

GRINTER, R. (1985) 'Bridging the Gulf: The need for an Anti-racist Multi-culturalism', *Multi-cultural Teaching*, Warwick, Trentham Books.

GRINTER, R. (1990) 'Developing an Anti-racist National Curriculum: Constraints and new directions', in PUMFREY, P.D. and VERMA, G.K. *Race Relations and Urban Education: Contexts and Promising Practices*, London, The Falmer Press.

HALSTEAD, J.M. (1986) *The Case for Muslim Voluntary-aided Schools: Some Philosophical Reflections*, Cambridge, Islamic Academy.

HAMILTON, D. (1980) 'Educational research and the shadows of Francis Galton and Ronald Fisher', in DOCKREL, W.B. and HAMILTON, D. (Eds) *Rethinking Educational Research*, London, Hodder and Stoughton.

HARGREAVES, D.H. (1980) 'Classroom studies', *Educational Analysis*, **2**, 2.

HASKEY, J. (1990) 'The ethnic minority populations of Great Britain: Estimates by ethnic group and country of birth', *Population Trends 60*, London, OPCS.

HULL, J. (1993) *The Fundamental Distinction: A Review of DFE Draft Circular X/94*, University of Birmingham.

INSTITUTE OF RACE RELATIONS (1982) *Roots of Racism*, London, Tavistock.

ISLAMIC ACADEMY (1985) *Swann Committee Report — An Evaluation from the Muslim Point of View*, Cambridge, Islamic Academy.

JEFFCOATE, R. (1984a) 'Ideologies and multi-cultural education', in CRAFT, M. (Ed) *Education and Cultural Pluralism*, London, The Falmer Press.

JEFFCOATE, R. (1984b) *Ethnic Minorities and Education*, London, Harper Education Series.

KALLOS, D. (1980) 'On educational phenomena and educational research', in DOCKREL, W.B. and HAMILTON, D. (Eds) *Rethinking Educational Research*, London, Hodder and Stoughton.

KELLY, E. and COHN, T. (1988) *Racism in Schools: New Research Evidence*, London, Trentham Books.

KELLY, E. (1989) 'The tip of the iceberg part 3', in MACDONALD, I. (Ed) *Murder in the Playground — The Report of Macdonald Inquiry into Racism and Racial Violence in Manchester Schools*, London, Longsight Press.

KELLY, E. (1990) 'Use and abuse of racial language in secondary schools', in PUMFREY, P.D. and VERMA, G.K. (Eds) *Race Relations and Urban Education: Contexts and Promising Practices*, London, The Falmer Press.

KHAN, S.V. (1979) *Minority Families in Britain*, London, Macmillan.

KIRP, D. (1979) *Doing Good By Doing Little — Race and Schooling in Britain*, London, University of California Press.

KING, R. (1979) 'Italians in Britain: And idiosyncratic immigration', *Journal of the Association of Teachers of Italian*, **29**, Autumn 1979 (quoted in DES, 1985).

LONGFORD, L.T. (1989) 'Variance component analysis', in SMITH, D.J. and TOMLINSON, S. (Eds) *The School Effect — A Study of Multi-racial Comprehensives*, London, Policy Studies Institute.

LYNCH, J. (1987) *Prejudice Reduction and the Schools*, London, Cassell.

LYNCH, J. (1989) 'International interdependence: Swann's contribution', in VERMA, G.K. (Ed) *Education for All — A Landmark in Pluralism*, Lewes, The Falmer Press.

MACDONALD, I. (1989) *Murder in the Playground — The Report of the Macdonald Inquiry into Racism and Racial Violence in Manchester Schools*, London, Longsight Press.

MANCHESTER LEA (1985) *Multifaith Manchester — Manchester City Council Agreed Syllabus for Religious Education*, Manchester City Council.

MEYER, V. (1982) 'King David High School Manchester: An introduction to its historical background and current role', in SKINNER, G. (Ed) *Issues in Contemporary Jewish Education in Britain*, Research Report, University of Manchester Department of Education.

MILES, R. (1984) 'Irish in the UK', in CASHMORE, E.E. (Ed) *Dictionary of Race and Ethnic Relations*, London, Routledge and Kegan Paul.

MILNER, D. (1975) *Children and Race*, Harmondsworth, Penguin.

MORTIMORE, P. *et al.* (1988) *School Matters: The Junior Years*, Wells, Open Books.

MULLARD, C. (1982) 'Multi-racial education in Britain: From assimilation to cultural pluralism', in TIERNEY, J. (Ed) *Race, Migration and Schooling*, Eastbourne, Holt Education.

MULLARD, C. (1984) *Anti-Racist Education: The Three'O's*, London, National Association for Multi-Racial Education.

MULLARD, C. (1985) 'A Critique of the Swann Report', UNIVERSITY OF BRADFORD, *Proceedings on The Swann Report: Conference and Seminar*, University of Bradford.

NEWHAM MONITORING PROJECT (1990) *Racism and Racist Violence in Schools*, London, Newham Monitoring Project Publications.

NISBET, J. (1980) 'Educational research: The state of the art', in DOCKREL, W.B. and HAMILTON, D. (Eds) *Rethinking Educational Research*, London, Hodder and Stoughton.

O'KEEFFE, B. (1986) *Faith, Culture and the Dual System: A Comparative Study of Church and County Schools*, London, The Falmer Press.

OPCS (1992) *Census Newsletter*, 19th March.

OWEN, D. (1992) *Ethnic Minorities in Great Britain: Settlement Patterns*, Warwick, University of Warwick.

PAREKH, B. (1990) 'Britain and the Social Logic of Pluralism', COMMISSION FOR RACIAL EQUALITY, *Britain: A Plural Society*, London, Commission for Racial Equality.

POWNEY, J. and WATTS, M. (1987) *Interviewing in Educational Research*, London, Routledge and Kegan Paul.

PUMFREY, P.D. and VERMA, G.K. (1990) *Race Relations and Urban Education: Contexts and Promising Practices*, London, The Falmer Press.

PUMFREY, P.D. and VERMA, G.K. (1993) *Cultural Diversity and the Curriculum* (4 volumes), London, The Falmer Press.

REX, J. (1989) 'Equality of opportunity, multi-culturalism, anti-racism and education for all', VERMA, G.K. (Ed) *Education for All — A Landmark in Pluralism*, Lewes, The Falmer Press.

REX, J. and TOMLINSON, S. (1979) *Colonial Immigrants in a British City*, London, Routledge and Kegan Paul.

RUTTER, M. *et al.* (1979) *Fifteen Thousand Hours*, Wells, Open Books.

SALFORD LEA (1987) *Religious Education — Planning and Practice*, Salford City Council.

SARWAR, G. (1991) *British Muslims and Schools: Proposals for Progress*, London, The Muslim Educational Trust.

SELKIRK, K.E. (1976) *Sampling* (Rediguide 4), Nottingham University.

SCOTT, S. (1985) 'Working through the contradictions in researching postgraduate education', in BURGESS, R.G. (Ed) *Field Methods in the Study of Education*, Lewes, The Falmer Press.

SELECT COMMITTEE (1973) *Education*, London, HMSO.

SHAW, C. (1988) 'Latest estimates of ethnic minority populations', *Population Trends*, London, Office of Population Censuses and Surveys.

SHAW, J. (1990) 'A strategy for improving race relations in urban education', in PUMFREY, P.D. and VERMA, G.K. (Ed) *Race Relations and Urban Education: Contexts and Promising Practices*, London, The Falmer Press.

SHERMAN, R. and WEBB, R. (Eds) (1988) *Qualitative Research in Education: Focus and Methods*, London, The Falmer Press.

SHIPMAN, M. (Ed) (1985) *Educational Research: Principles, Polices and Practices*, London, The Falmer Press.

SKINNER, G. (1980) 'Faith and Education — A Study of Alternative Models', Lancaster University DASE dissertation (unpublished).

SKINNER, G. (1982) *Issues in Contemporary Jewish Education in Britain*, Research Report, University of Manchester Department of Education.

SKINNER, G. (1990) 'Religion, Culture and Education', in PUMFREY, P.D. and VERMA, G.K. (Ed) *Race Relations and Urban Education: Contexts and Promising Practices*, London, The Falmer Press.

SMITH, D.J. and TOMLINSON, S. (1989) *The School Effect — A Study of Multi-racial Comprehensives*, London, Policy Studies Institute.

SMITH, J.K. and HESHUSIUS, L. (1986) 'Closing down the conversation: The end of the quantitative-qualitative debate among educational inquirers', *Educational Researcher*, **15**, 1, pp. 4–12.

SPENCER (1987) 'Racist Names Hurt More than Sticks and Stones', London, *The Times Educational Supplement*, 18 September.

STONE, M. (1981) *The Education of the Black Child in Britain: The Myth of Multi-racial Education*, London, Fontana.

STONE, S. and PUMFREY, P.D. (1990) 'The child using English as a second language and the National Curriculum 5–11', in PUMFREY, P.D. and VERMA, G.K. (1990) *Race Relations and Urban Education: Contexts and Promising Practices*, London, The Falmer Press.

TATTUM, D.P. and LANE, D.A. (Eds) (1989) *Bullying in School*, London, Trentham Books.

THE LINGUISTICS MINORITY PROJECT (1984) 'Bilingualism and mother tongue teaching in England', in CRAFT, M. (Ed) *Education and Cultural Pluralism*, London, The Falmer Press.

THOMAS, K. (1984) 'Inter-cultural relations in the classroom', in CRAFT, M. (Ed) *Education and Cultural Pluralism*, London, The Falmer Press.

TIERNEY, J. (Ed) (1984) *Race, Migration and Schooling*, London, Holt Education.

TIMES EDUCATIONAL SUPPLEMENT (1994) 'Racial Attacks Drive Pupils Out', 25.2.94.

TOMLINSON, S. (1983) *Ethnic Minorities in British Schools — A Review of the Literature 1960–1982*, London, Heinemann Educational Books.

TOMLINSON, S. (1989) 'The origins of the ethnocentric curriculum', in VERMA, G.K. (Ed) *Education for All — A Landmark in Pluralism*, Lewes, The Falmer Press.

TOMLINSON, S. (1990) 'Race relations and the urban context', in PUMFREY, P.D. and VERMA, G.K. (Eds) *Race Relations and Urban Education: Contexts and Promising Practices*, London, The Falmer Press.

TROYNA, B. (1978) 'Race and streaming: A case study', *Educational Review*, **30**.

TROYNA, B. (1984a) 'Immigration Laws: UK', in CASHMORE, E.E. (Ed) *Dictionary of Race and Ethnic Relations*, London, Routledge and Kegan Paul.

TROYNA, B. (1984b) 'Powell, Enoch', in CASHMORE, E.E. (Ed) *Dictionary of Race and Ethnic Relations*, London, Routledge and Kegan Paul.

TROYNA, B. (1989) 'A New Planet? Tackling Racial Inequality in All-white Schools and Colleges', in VERMA, G.K. (Ed) *Education for All — A Landmark in Pluralism*, London, The Falmer Press.

TROYNA, B. and CARRINGTON, B. (1990) *Education, Racism and Reform*, London, Routledge.

TROYNA, B. (1991) 'Children, race and racism: The limitations of research and policy', *British Journal of Educational Studies*, **Vol. XXXIX**, No. 4.

UNIVERSITY OF BRADFORD (1985) *Proceedings on The Swann Report: Conference and Seminar*, University of Bradford.

VERMA, G.K. (Ed) (1989) *Education for All — A Landmark in Pluralism*, London, The Falmer Press.

VERMA, G.K. (1990) 'Pluralism: Some theoretical and practical considerations', *Britain: A Plural Society*, Report of a seminar, London, Commission for Racial Equality.

VERMA, G.K. (1992) 'Cultural diversity in secondary schools: Its nature, extent and curricular implications', in PUMFREY, P.D. and VERMA, G.K. (1992) (Eds) *Cultural Diversity and the National Curriculum: Volume 1 — The Foundation Subjects and RE in Secondary Schools*, London, The Falmer Press.

VERMA, G.K. with ASHWORTH, B. (1986) *Ethnicity and Educational Achievement in British Schools*, London, Macmillan.

VERMA, G.K. and BAGLEY, C. (1984) *Race Relations and Cultural Differences*, London, Croom Helm.

VERMA, G.K. and DARBY, D.S. (1990) 'Race relations and the media', in PUMFREY, P.D. and VERMA, G.K. (Eds) *Race Relations and Urban Education: Contexts and Promising Practices*, London, The Falmer Press.

VERMA, G.K. and DARBY, D.S. (1994) *Winners and Losers: Ethnic Minorities in Sport and Recreation*, London, The Falmer Press.

VISRAM, R. (1986) *Ayahs, Lascars and Princes — Indians in Britain 1700–1947*, London, Pluto Press.

VYAS, H.V. (1983) 'Gujaratis in Britain: Adaption and assertion', *Gujarat Samachar*, 13 May 1983.

WATERS, H. (1992) 'Race, culture and interpersonal conflict', *International Journal of Inter-cultural Relations*, **16**.

WILLIAMS, S. (1989) Foreword to VERMA, G.K. (Ed) *Education for All — A Landmark in Pluralism*, Lewes, The Falmer Press.

WILLEY, R. (1984) 'Policy Responses in Education', in CRAFT, M. (Ed) *Education and Cultural Pluralism*, London, The Falmer Press.

WIRTH, F.M. (1976) quoted in LYNCH, J. (1989) 'International Interdependence: Swann's Contribution', in VERMA, G.K. (Ed) *Education for All — A Landmark in Pluralism*, London, The Falmer Press.

WIRTH, F.M. (1979) 'Ethnic minorities and school policy in Europe', *Comparative Education Review*, **23**, 1.

WOODS, P. (1979) *The Divided School*, London, Routledge and Kegan Paul.

WOODS, P. (1986) *Inside Schools — Ethnography in Educational Research*, London, Routledge and Kegan Paul.

WOODS, P. (1988) 'Educational Ethnography in Britain', in SHERMAN, R. and WEBB, R. (Eds) *Qualitative Research in Education: Focus and Methods*, Lewes, The Falmer Press.

WRAGG, E.C. (1976) *Conducting and Analysing Interviews*, Nottingham University.

WRIGHT, C. (1992) *Race Relations in the Primary School*, London, David Fulton.

WROE, M. (1991) 'Sunrise by Satellite for Europe's Asians', *The Independent*, Wednesday 14 August 1991, p. 17.

ZEC, P. (1981) 'Multi-cultural education: What kind of relativism is possible?', in JAMES, A. and JEFFCOATE, R. (Eds) *The School in the Multi-cultural Society*, London, Harper and Row.

ZEC, P. (1983) 'Dealing with racial incidents in schools', in FIGUEROA, P. and FYFE, A. (Eds) *Education for Cultural Diversity*, London, Routledge.

Appendices

Appendix 1

Teacher Interview Schedule

INTER-ETHNIC RELATIONSHIPS IN SECONDARY SCHOOLS
Teacher Interview Schedule

School _____ Date _____

A.1   Name _____

A.2   Sex   A.3   Age Under 26   26–35   36–45   46–55   over 55

A.4   Department and position held

A.5   Number of Years in the School   _____

A.6   How would you describe your ethnicity or ethnic group?

A.7   Do you speak any languages other than English?

Previous Experience and Initial Training

B.1   Have you had any previous teaching or other experience which has influenced your understanding of ethnic minority pupils or multi-cultural practice?

Initial Training

College/University and dates:

Main course subjects for initial training:

B.2   How effective was your initial training in preparing you for teaching in a multi-racial school?
[ ] VERY   [ ] REASONABLY   [ ] NOT VERY   [ ] NOT AT ALL
(Explore)

TEACHER INTERVIEW Page 1 of 8

REF ___ / ___ / ___

Externally Organised INSET

C.1 Please give brief details of any recent INSET or courses of further study attended <u>not</u> explicitly on multi-cultural or anti-racist issues and organised by <u>outside bodies</u> (e.g. LEA). [Brief details of up to 2]

   a.

   b.

C.2 To what extent did the course(s) take account of multi-cultural/anti-racist matters?

	A LOT	SOME	VERY LITTLE	NOT AT ALL
a.	[ ]	[ ]	[ ]	[ ]
b.	[ ]	[ ]	[ ]	[ ]

C.3 Have you attended any externally organised INSET courses on multi-cultural or anti-racist issues? (If 'No', go to D.1)   [ ] YES   [ ] NO

C.4 When was it? _____

C.5 Who provided it? _____

C.6 Describe briefly how the course was structured

C.7 To what extent did the course affect:

   a. your understanding of ethnic minority communities
   A LOT [ ]   SOME [ ]   VERY LITTLE [ ]   NOT AT ALL [ ]

   b. your awareness of multi-cultural/anti-racist issues in education
   A LOT [ ]   SOME [ ]   VERY LITTLE [ ]   NOT AT ALL [ ]

   c. your self-awareness in such areas
   A LOT [ ]   SOME [ ]   VERY LITTLE [ ]   NOT AT ALL [ ]

   d. your ability to respond as a teacher
   A LOT [ ]   SOME [ ]   VERY LITTLE [ ]   NOT AT ALL [ ]

Any further comments on the course?

C.8 Did the school draw on your experiences gained on the course?
A LOT [ ]   SOME [ ]   VERY LITTLE [ ]   NOT AT ALL [ ]

Details of school response:

Internally Organised INSET

D.1 Please give brief details of any recent INSET attended not explicitly on multi-cultural or anti-racist issues and organised by the school. [Brief details of up to 2]

a.

b.

D.2 To what extent did the course(s) take account of multi-cultural/anti-racist matters?

	A LOT	SOME	VERY LITTLE	NOT AT ALL
a.	[ ]	[ ]	[ ]	[ ]
b.	[ ]	[ ]	[ ]	[ ]

D.3 Have you attended any school-based INSET courses on multi-cultural or anti-racist issues? (If 'No', go to E.1)   [ ] YES   [ ] NO

D.4 When was it? _____

D.5 Who was responsible for setting it up?

D.6 Describe briefly how the course was structured

TEACHER INTERVIEW Page 3 of 8

REF ___ / ___ / ___

D.7 To what extent did the course affect:
a. your understanding of ethnic minority communities
A LOT [ ]   SOME [ ]   VERY LITTLE [ ]   NOT AT ALL [ ]

b. your awareness of multi-cultural/anti-racist issues in education
A LOT [ ]   SOME [ ]   VERY LITTLE [ ]   NOT AT ALL [ ]

c. your self-awareness in such areas
A LOT [ ]   SOME [ ]   VERY LITTLE [ ]   NOT AT ALL [ ]

d. your ability to respond as a teacher
A LOT [ ]   SOME [ ]   VERY LITTLE [ ]   NOT AT ALL [ ]

Any further comments on the course?

D.8 Did the school use, develop or reinforce what you learnt on the course?

REF ___ / ___ / ___

Policy

E.1   Does your LEA have a policy on multi-cultural/anti-racist education or equal opportunities? (If 'No' go to E.3)
[ ] YES   [ ] NO   [ ] DON'T KNOW

E.2   What is your evaluation of the policy itself? (I'm going to ask you about the way it has worked in school later)

E.3   Does your SCHOOL have a policy on multi-cultural/anti-racist education or equal opportunities? (If 'No' go to E.7)
[ ] YES   [ ] NO   [ ] DON'T KNOW

E.4   Who was involved in its production?
ALL STAFF [ ]   SENIOR STAFF [ ]   HEAD ONLY [ ]
WORKING GROUP [ ]
OTHER [ ] (details) _____

E.5   What is your evaluation of the effectiveness of the policy?

E.6   How do you think other staff have responded to the policy?

E.7   Are there sections of the general school policy which deal with similar issues?

E.8   What value do you think policies have in improving inter-ethnic understanding or relationships in the school?
[ ] NONE   [ ] VERY LITTLE [ ]   [ ] SOME   [ ] A LOT   (Explore)

REF ___ / ___ / ___

Teacher's Role

F.1　Are there any ways in which you see the <u>curriculum</u> contributing to the pupils' knowledge and understanding of other cultures or communities?

F.2　Are there any ways in which you see the curriculum contributing to better inter-ethnic <u>relationships</u> in the school?
(If 'Yes' ask for <u>evidence</u> and examples)

F.3　Are there other ways in which teachers are able to contribute to good inter-ethnic relationships in the school?

Pupils

G.1　How would you describe the ethnic composition of the school?

G.2　Do you feel that children from any particular ethnic background do better or less well than others in some subject(s) (If 'yes' explore further)

G.3　To what extent do children from the different ethnic groups mix with each other in school (e.g. in class, school societies, playground etc.)
[ ] A LOT　[ ] TO SOME EXTENT　[ ] NOT MUCH　[ ] NOT AT ALL (Explore)

G.4　Would you say that the degree of mixing is increasing or decreasing?
[ ] INCREASING　[ ] DECREASING　[ ] SAME
(Reasons?)

G.5   Does the school make any particular provision for pupils from any ethnic, linguistic or religious groups?
[ ] YES   [ ] NO   [ ] DON'T KNOW

G.6   Have there been any requests for such provision from the community or pupils? (If 'Yes' explore)
[ ] YES   [ ] NO   [ ] DON'T KNOW

G.7   To what extent can such provisions help or hinder inter-ethnic relationships in school?

G.8   How well do you think students in school know about each other's cultures or communities?

G.9   How would you describe the state of inter-ethnic relationships in this school in general?
[ ] V. GOOD [ ] GOOD [ ] SATISFACTORY [ ] POOR
[ ] V. POOR

G.10   Does the school have any policy for dealing with racial incidents? (If 'Yes' ask for details).
[ ] YES   [ ] NO   [ ] DON'T KNOW

G.11   What examples would you give which illustrate good inter-ethnic relationships in this school?

G.12   Can you give any examples or illustrations of bad inter-ethnic relationships?

REF ___ / ___ / ___

The Community
H.1   How would you describe the communities in the catchment area of the school?

H.2   What links does the school have with these communities?

H.3   How effective are these links in producing good relationships in school?

H.4   What are relationships like between different communities outside school?

H.5   To what extent do these relationships influence pupil relationships in school?

Additional Comments
I.1   Is there anything else you would like to add about your views on inter-ethnic relationships and education in general or in this school specifically?

Appendix 2

Student Interview Schedule

REF ___ / ___ / ___

INTER-ETHNIC RELATIONSHIPS IN SECONDARY SCHOOLS
Student Interview Schedule

School _____

Name_____   <u>Sex</u> M F <u>Age</u> _____

Biographical Details
A.1   What communities or religious groups do you belong to?
       [Prompt with e.g. if necessary]

       a.   _____

       b.   _____

       c.   _____

A.2   Where were you born? [If Britain go to A.4] _____

A.3   How long have you lived in Britain? _____

A.4   Have you been to school in any other country?   YES [   ]   NO [   ]
       [If Yes, explore]

A.5   Can you tell me where your Mum or Dad was born? _____
                                                         _____

Language
B.1   Which language(s) do you know other than English?

       a.   _____

       b.   _____

       c.   _____

B.2   Which language do you normally speak at home? _____
B.3   Which language do you normally use when you are talking with your friends

       in school? _____ [If English, go to C1]
B.4   What do other people say about you using this language in school?

STUDENT INTERVIEW Page 1 of 6

REF ___ / ___ / ___

Social Involvement

C.1 Do you belong to any clubs or societies outside school?

NO [ ]   YES [ ]   DETAILS _____

C.2 Do you belong to any clubs, societies or sports teams in school?

NO [ ]   YES [ ]   DETAILS _____
(Explore problems of involvement, opportunities, etc.)

C.3 Have you been on any school trips, holidays or field courses?

NO [ ]   YES [ ]   DETAILS _____
(Explore problems, opportunities, etc.)

School Work

D.1 What is your favourite subject? _____
D.2 Are there subjects you like to do and cannot?

NO [ ]   YES [ ] _____
(Explore reasons)

D.3 Are there any subjects you dislike doing?

NO [ ]   YES [ ]
(Explore reasons)

D.4 Do you learn in school about what is going on in other parts of the world today?

A LOT [ ]   SOME [ ]   NOT MUCH [ ]   NOT AT ALL [ ]
(Example?)

STUDENT INTERVIEW Page 2 of 6

REF ___ / ___ / ___

D.5 Do you learn in school about the beliefs or lifestyles of the different groups of pupils in school?
A LOT [ ]   SOME [ ]   NOT MUCH [ ]   NOT AT ALL [ ]
(Example?)

D.6 Do you learn in school about how different groups of people in Britain live?
A LOT [ ]   SOME [ ]   NOT MUCH [ ]   NOT AT ALL [ ]
(Example?)

D.7 Do you learn in school about how to get on with other people?
A LOT [ ]   SOME [ ]   NOT MUCH [ ]   NOT AT ALL [ ]
(Example?)

Relationships

E.1 Who are your best friends at school? In what ways are they like you or different from you?

E.2 Who are your best friends out of school?

E.3 Are there any students in school who you don't ever talk with or do things with?
NO [ ]   YES [ ]
(If YES, explore reasons)

STUDENT INTERVIEW Page 3 of 6

REF ___ / ___ / ___

E.4 Do you ever feel you are treated badly in school?
NEVER [ ]   RARELY [ ]   SOMETIMES [ ]   ALL THE TIME [ ]
(Explore)

E.5 Are there any other pupils who are ever treated badly?
NONE [ ]   A FEW [ ]   A LOT [ ]
(Explore details/reasons)

E.6 Would you say that discipline in your school is too strict, not strict enough or about right?
TOO STRICT [ ]   RIGHT [ ]   NOT STRICT ENOUGH [ ]

E.7 Do you ever get called names which you don't like in school?
NEVER [ ]   RARELY [ ]   SOMETIMES [ ]   ALL THE TIME [ ]
If NEVER go to E.8
Why do you get called names?

What do teachers do about this?

E.8 Do other pupils ever get called names which they don't like?
NEVER [ ]   RARELY [ ]   SOMETIMES [ ]   ALL THE TIME [ ]
If NEVER go to E.9
Why are they called names?

What do you think about this?

Do you ever call other students names which they don't like?

STUDENT INTERVIEW Page 4 of 6

REF ___ / ___ / ___

E.9   Do people ever tell jokes in school about your religion or race or colour?
NEVER [ ]   RARELY [ ]   SOMETIMES [ ]   ALL THE TIME [ ]
If NEVER go to E.10
Why do you think they tell these jokes?

How do you feel about it?

E.10   Do people in school ever tell jokes about other students' religion, race or colour?
NEVER [ ]   RARELY [ ]   SOMETIMES [ ]   ALL THE TIME [ ]
If NEVER go to E.11
Why do you think they tell these jokes?

How do you think the students being joked about feel?

Do you ever tell jokes like this?
(Explore)

E.11   Have you ever been bullied by anyone in school?
NO [ ] (If No, go to E.12)   YES [ ]
Why do you think the other pupil(s) picked on you?

Was enough done to stop it?

E.12   Have you ever been told off for bullying?
NO [ ]   YES [ ]
(If YES explore)

STUDENT INTERVIEW Page 5 of 6

REF ___ / ___ / ___

E.13   Do you know what we mean by good 'race relations'?
       Do you think your school can be described as having good race relations?
       (Probe reasons)
       VERY GOOD [ ]   GOOD [ ]   POOR [ ]   VERY POOR [ ]

E.14   Does the school have rules or regulations to encourage good race relations?

E.15   Does the school do anything else to help pupils to get on with each other?

E.16   What do you like most about being at this school?

E.17   What do you dislike most about being at this school?

Final Question
F.1   Is there anything else you would like to say to me about the things we have
       discussed or about the school?

STUDENT INTERVIEW Page 6 of 6

Appendix 3

Questionnaire

Relationships in School
Some Questions

The Questions on this form are mainly about school and how people in school get on with each other.

It is not an exam or test. There are no right or wrong answers.

Please answer each question by yourself as carefully and honestly as you can.

We do not want you to put your name on the form. Once you have handed it in, nobody will know that this is your form.

When you have finished, please read through your answers one more time in case you want to change or add anything.

University of Manchester
Christ Church College of Higher Education
Canterbury

1. How old are you? _____ years

2. Please tick one box: Male ☐ Female ☐

3. These are some of the ways people in Britain might describe themselves. If you would describe yourself in any of these ways, please tick the box

You may tick more than one box ☑

☐ African	☐ Indian
☐ Arab	☐ Irish
☐ Asian	☐ Italian
☐ Bangladeshi	☐ Jewish
☐ Black African	☐ Pakistani
☐ British	☐ Polish
☐ Caribbean	☐ Scottish
☐ Chinese	☐ Traveller
☐ East African Asian	☐ Turkish
☐ English	☐ Vietnamese
☐ Greek	☐ Welsh

If you would describe yourself in a way not listed, please write it here:

_____

Please turn to next page

4. These are some **religious** communities in Britain. If you feel that you belong to one, please tick the box. ☑

    ☐ I do not feel as if I belong to <u>any</u> religious community

    ☐ Buddhist

    ☐ Christian

    ☐ Hindu

    ☐ Jewish

    ☐ Muslim

    ☐ Rastafarian

    ☐ Sikh

    Do you belong to a religious community or group not in this list? If so, please write the name here.

    _____

Please turn to next page

5. These are some of the **languages** which are spoken in Britain. If any are yours, please tick the box. ☑

   You may tick more than one box.
   Please do not tick boxes of languages you have <u>only</u> learnt as a school subject.

☐ Arabic	☐ Hindi
☐ Bengali	☐ Italian
☐ Cantonese	☐ Pashto
☐ Caribbean English	☐ Polish
☐ Creole/Patois	☐ Punjabi
☐ English	☐ Spanish
☐ Gaelic/Gallic	☐ Turkish
☐ Greek	☐ Urdu
☐ Gujarati	☐ Vietnamese
☐ Hakka	☐ Welsh
☐ Hebrew	☐ Yiddish

   Do you speak a language which is not in this list? If you do, please write the name here.

   _____

   Please turn to next page

6. Please think about students in your year who belong to communities or religious groups which are **different** from yours.

   How much do you think you know about the beliefs and the lifestyles of their communities or groups?

   Please tick the box which is closest to your answer. ☑

   ☐ I know a lot about most of them

   ☐ I know a lot about some of them but not others

   ☐ I know quite a bit about most of them

   ☐ I don't know very much about them

   ☐ I don't know anything about them

7. How much do you think they know about **your** beliefs and the way **you** live your life?

   Please tick the box which is closest to your answer ☑

   ☐ They know a lot

   ☐ They know quite a bit

   ☐ They don't know very much

   ☐ They don't know anything

8. How much do you think most of your teachers do to help you understand about the different beliefs or backgrounds of students in school?

   Please tick the box which is closest to your answer ☑

   ☐ Most teachers do a lot

   ☐ Most teachers do quite a bit

   ☐ Most teachers don't do very much

   ☐ Most teachers don't do anything

Please turn to next page

9. In general, how well do students from different backgrounds or religions get on with each other in school?

   Please tick the box which is closest to your answer. ☑

   ☐ In general they get on very well

   ☐ In general they get on quite well

   ☐ In general they don't get on well

   ☐ In general they don't get on at all

10. Do you sometimes get called names which you don't like in school?

    Please tick the box which is closest to your answer. ☑

    ☐ Never, **If you tick this box please go straight on to question 13**

    ☐ Not very often

    ☐ Quite a lot

    ☐ All the time

11. If you are called names which you don't like, what are they usually about?

    You may tick more than one box ☑

    ☐ Because I am a girl

    ☐ Because I am a boy

    ☐ Because of my religion

    ☐ Because of my race or colour

    ☐ Because of the language I speak

    ☐ Another reason. **If you want to**, write it here

    _____

    _____

    Please turn to next page

12. If you are called names which you don't like, how does it make you feel?

You may tick more than one box ☑

☐ It doesn't really bother me

☐ I feel very sad

☐ I feel very angry

☐ I feel left out

☐ I feel like getting my own back

13. In school, do **you** ever call other people names which **they** don't like?

Please tick the box which is closest to your answer. ☑

☐ Never. **If you tick this box, please go straight on to question 16**

☐ Not very often

☐ Quite a lot

☐ All the time

14. If you do call other people names, what are they usually about?

You may tick more than one box ☑

☐ Because they are a girl

☐ Because they are a boy

☐ Because of their religion

☐ Because of their race or colour

☐ Because of the language they speak

☐ Another reason. **If you want to**, write it here.

_____

Please turn to next page

15. If you do call other people names which they don't like, how do you think they feel?

    You may tick more than one box ☑

    ☐ It doesn't really bother them

    ☐ They feel very sad

    ☐ They feel very angry

    ☐ They feel left out

    ☐ They feel like getting their own back

16. Do people in school from communities or religions different from yours sometimes tell jokes about your race or religion or colour?

    Please tick the box which is closest to your answer. ☑

    ☐ Never. **If you tick this box, please go straight on to question 18**

    ☐ Not very often

    ☐ Quite a lot

    ☐ All the time

17. If people do sometimes tell jokes like this, how do you feel?

    You may tick more than one box ☑

    ☐ I just ignore them

    ☐ I usually find the jokes funny

    ☐ I feel sad

    ☐ I feel angry

    ☐ I feel left out

    ☐ I try to get my own back

Please turn to next page

18. Do **you** sometimes tell jokes about other students' race or religion or colour?

   Please tick the box which is closest to your answer. ☑

   ☐ Never. **If you tick this box, please go straight on to question 20**

   ☐ Not very often

   ☐ Quite a lot

   ☐ All the time

19. If you do sometimes tell jokes like this, how do you think **they** feel?

   You may tick more than one box ☑

   ☐ They just ignore them

   ☐ They usually find the jokes funny

   ☐ They feel sad

   ☐ They feel angry

   ☐ They feel left out

   ☐ They try to get their own back

20. Do you ever get bullied in school?

   Please tick the box which is closest to your answer. ☑

   ☐ Never. **If you tick this box, please go straight on to question 22**

   ☐ Sometimes

   ☐ Quite a lot

   ☐ All the time

Please turn to the next page

21. If you are bullied, what is usually the reason?

    You may tick more than one box. ☑

    ☐ Because I am a girl

    ☐ Because I am a boy

    ☐ Because of my age

    ☐ Because of my religion

    ☐ Because of my race or colour

    ☐ Because of the language I speak

    ☐ Another reason. **If you want to**, write it here.

    _____

22. Do you ever bully other students in school?

    Please tick the box which is closest to your answer. ☑

    ☐ Never. **If you tick this box, please go straight on to question 24**

    ☐ Sometimes

    ☐ Quite a lot

    ☐ All the time

23. If you do bully other students, what is usually the reason?

    You may tick more than one box ☑

    ☐ Because they are a girl

    ☐ Because they are a boy

    ☐ Because of their age

    ☐ Because of their religion

    ☐ Because of their race or colour

    ☐ Because of the language

    ☐ Another reason. **If you want to**, write it here.

    _____

    Please turn to the next page

24. Please write here what you like most about school.

_____

_____

_____

_____

_____

25. Please write here what you dislike most about school.

_____

_____

_____

_____

_____

26. If there is anything else you would like to say about your school or the different groups in it, please write it here.

_____

_____

_____

_____

_____

There are no more questions to answer.

Thank you for filling in this form.

Before you hand in the form, please read through your answers one more time to check if you want to change any of them or add anything.

Appendix 4

Questionnaire Results

PART A provides tables with simple scores for the total sample.

PART B gives more detailed analysis of scores according to particular groupings. While the analysis of the data allowed for a wide range of comparisons between ethnic, religious and linguistic groups, the inclusion of all these results here would be impossible. We have therefore selected those comparisons which have provided the most interesting patterns and which are referred to in the text. In addition to comparison between the result for all ethnic minority students and all others, comparisons are provided for two ethnic identities (Caribbean and Bangladeshi) and one religious identity (Muslim). Where patterns are statistically significant at or above the 99 per cent level of certainty they are indicated*.

PART A
Questionnaire Results for All Schools

Total Number of responses: 2,326 (111 in Bengali, 3 in Turkish)

1. **Age Range**
   Age 12:459   Age 13:757   Age 14:393   Age 15:656   Age 16:17
   Missing: 44

2. **Gender**
   Male: 1,241 (53.4%)   Female: 1,038 (44.6%)   Missing: 47

3. **Communities**
   Pupils were allowed to tick more than one community.

Community	Responses	Percentage
African	81	3.5
Arab	31	1.3
Asian	156	6.7
Bangladeshi	254	10.9
Black African	44	1.9
British	1,400	60.2
Caribbean	153	6.6
Chinese	25	1.1
East African Asian	299	12.9
English	1,320	56.7
Greek	46	2.0
Indian	123	15.3
Irish	95	4.1
Italian	27	1.2
Jewish	26	1.1
Pakistani	110	4.7
Polish	20	0.9
Scottish	74	3.2
Traveller	7	0.3
Turkish	46	2.0
Vietnamese	10	0.4
Welsh	55	2.4

Additional communities written in by pupils:

Bengali	13	0.6
White	13	0.6
European	7	0.3
Mixed race	71	1.3
Spanish	4	0.2

4. Religious communities

Community	Responses	Percentage
I don't belong to any	696	29.9
Buddhist	27	1.2
Christian	840	36.1
Hindu	62	2.7
Jewish	16	0.7
Muslim	492	21.2
Rastafarian	11	0.5
Sikh	15	0.6
Nil response	167	7.2

Specific religious communities added by pupils:

Catholic	26	1.1
Greek Orthodox	9	0.4
Spiritualist	6	0.3
Jehovah's Witness	9	0.4

5. Languages (Pupils were allowed to tick more than one language).

Language	Responses	Percentage
Arabic	91	3.9
Bengali	256	11.0
Cantonese	23	1.0
Caribbean English	88	3.8
Creole/Patois	53	2.3
English	1,868	80.3
Gaelic/Gallic	16	0.7
Greek	49	2.1
Gujarati	103	4.4
Hakka	2	0.1
Hebrew	10	0.4
Hindi	71	3.1
Italian	22	0.9
Pashto	5	0.2
Polish	7	0.3
Punjabi	103	4.4
Spanish	50	2.1
Turkish	39	1.7
Urdu	131	5.6
Vietnamese	9	0.4
Welsh	17	0.7
Yiddish	6	0.3

Additional languages mentioned:

Other European	95	4.1
Far Eastern	14	0.6
African	23	1.0
South Asian	8	0.3
Middle Eastern	3	0.1

6. Perception of the student's knowledge of other pupils

Answer	Responses	Percentage
I know a lot about most	148	6.4
I know a lot about some	402	17.3
I know quite a bit about most	764	32.8
I don't know very much	793	34.1
I don't know anything	179	7.7
Answers missing:	38	1.6

7. Perception of other students' knowledge of them

Answer	Responses	Percentage
They know a lot	279	12.0
They know quite a bit	1,106	47.5
They don't know very much	684	29.4
They don't know anything	198	8.5
Answers missing	57	2.5

8. Perception of help given by teachers to increase understanding

Answer	Responses	Percentage
Most teachers do a lot	461	19.8
Most teachers do quite a bit	987	21.5
Most teachers don't do very much	613	26.4
Teachers don't do anything	226	9.7
Answers missing	39	1.6

9. Perception of inter-ethnic relationships

Answer	Responses	Percentage
They get on very well	664	28.5
They get on quite well	1,370	58.9
They don't get on well	204	8.8
They don't get on at all	54	2.3
Answers missing	34	1.5

10. Frequency of being called names

Answer	Responses	Percentage
Never	503	21.6
Not very often	1,381	59.4
Quite a lot	314	13.5
All the time	94	4.0
Missing answers	34	1.5
Subset reporting some name-calling	1,789	76.9

11. The reasons for being called names

Answer	Responses	Percentage of sample	Percentage of subset
Because I am a girl	202	8.7	11.3
Because I am a boy	94	4.0	5.3
Because of my religion	191	8.2	10.7
Because of my race/colour	437	18.8	24.4
Because of my language	162	7.0	9.1
Another specific reason given			
To do with looks or features	282	12.1	15.8
For no specific reason	109	4.7	6.1
To do with dress/appearance	87	3.7	4.9
Not taken seriously	68	2.9	3.8
To do with their name	57	2.5	3.2
To do with their background	45	1.9	2.5
To do with work, 'swot', etc.	17	0.7	1.0
Things which aren't true about them	16	0.7	0.9

12. Feelings about name-calling

Answer	Responses	Percentage of sample	Percentage of subset
It doesn't really bother me	1,062	54.2	59.4
I feel very sad	207	8.9	11.6
I feel very angry	407	17.5	22.8
I feel left out	169	7.3	9.4
I feel like getting my own back	500	21.5	27.9

13. Frequency of student calling others names

Answer	Responses	Percentage
Never	601	25.8
Not very often	1,451	62.4

Quite a lot	163	7.0
All the time	64	2.8
Missing answers:	47	2.0
Subset of those who call names	1,678	72.1

14. Reasons for calling others names

Answer	Responses	Percentage of sample	Percentage of subset
Because they are a girl	99	4.3	5.9
Because they are a boy	128	5.5	7.6
Because of their religion	123	5.3	7.3
Because of their race or colour	182	7.8	10.8
Because of the language they speak	128	5.5	7.6
Other reasons mentioned			
Getting my own back	378	16.3	22.5
For no specific reason	184	7.9	11.0
Not serious/just fun	124	5.3	7.4
Size, looks, etc.	100	4.3	6.0
Another aspect of their background	40	1.7	2.4
To do with dress/appearance	32	1.4	1.9
To do with their name	29	1.2	1.7

15. Student's perception of the feelings of those being called names

Answer	Responses	Percentage of sample	Percentage of subset
It doesn't really bother them	728	31.3	43.4
They feel very sad	336	14.4	20.0
They feel very angry	371	16.0	22.1
They feel left out	197	8.5	11.7
They feel like getting their own back	529	22.7	31.5

16. Frequency of jokes told about the student's race, religion or colour?

Answer	Responses	Percentage
Never	805	34.6
Not very often	1,055	45.4
Quite a lot	318	13.7
All the time	72	3.1
Answers missing	76	3.2
Subset of those who have jokes told about them to some extent	1,445	62.1

17. Feelings of the student

Answer	Responses	Percentage of sample	Percentage of subset
I just ignore them	757	32.5	52.4
I usually find the jokes funny	592	25.5	41.0
I feel sad	102	4.4	7.1
I feel angry	212	9.1	14.7
I feel left out	54	2.3	3.7
I try to get my own back	219	9.4	15.2

18. Frequency of telling jokes about other students' race/religion/colour

Answer	Responses	Percentage
Never	1,188	51.1
Not very often	926	39.8
Quite a lot	121	5.2
All the time	31	1.3
Missing answers	60	2.6
Subset of students who tell jokes	1,078	46.3

19. Perception of how other students feel

Answer	Responses	Percentage of sample	Percentage of subset
They just ignore them	360	15.5	33.4
They usually find the jokes funny	508	21.8	47.1
They feel sad	186	8.0	17.3
They feel angry	194	8.3	18.0
They feel left out	88	3.8	8.2
They try to get their own back	233	10.0	21.6

20. Frequency of being bullied

Answer	Responses	Percentage
Never	1,332	57.3
Sometimes	797	34.3
Quite a lot	90	3.9
All the time	41	1.8
Missing answers	66	2.8
Subset of students bullied	928	39.9

21. Reasons for being bullied

Answer	Responses	Percentage of sample	Percentage of subset
Because I am a girl	102	4.4	11.0
Because I am a boy	44	1.9	4.7
Because of my age	116	5.0	12.5
Because of my religion	83	3.6	8.9
Because of my race or colour	205	8.5	22.1
Because of the language I speak	65	2.8	7.0
Another reason given			
For no specific reason	152	6.5	16.4
To do with looks or features	102	4.4	11.0
To do with their background	65	2.8	7.0
Not taken seriously	37	1.6	4.0
Pupils getting their own back	35	1.5	3.8
To do with dress/appearance	13	0.6	1.4
To do with work, 'swot', etc.	8	0.3	0.9
To do with extracting money	8	0.3	0.9

22. Frequency of bullying other students

Answer	Responses	Percentage
Never	1,588	68.3
Sometimes	583	25.1
Quite a lot	34	1.5
All the time	16	0.7
Missing answers	105	4.4
Subset of those bullying	633	27.2

23. Reasons for bullying

Answer	Responses	Percentage of sample	Percentage of subset
Because they are a girl	37	1.6	5.8
Because they are a boy	59	2.5	9.3
Because of their age	66	2.8	10.4
Because of their religion	37	1.6	5.8
Because of their race or colour	71	3.1	11.2
Because of the language they speak	42	1.8	6.6
Another specific reason given			
To do with looks or features	24	1.0	3.8
For no specific reason	64	2.8	10.1
To do with dress/appearance	4	0.2	0.6

To do with an aspect of background	26	1.1	4.1
Not done seriously	50	2.1	7.9
In retaliation	155	6.7	24.5

24. Please write here what you like most about your school
  (x1.1 for percentage of 2,134 pupils responding)

		Percentage
No comment	192	8.3
Nothing	74	3.2
Friends	944	40.6
Teachers in general	142	6.1
Some (e.g. specific) teachers	253	11.0
Lessons in general	192	8.3
Some (e.g. specific) lessons	699	30.1
General ethos	256	11.0
General relationships	111	4.8
Quality or range of lessons	220	9.5
Quality or range of facilities	189	8.1
Buildings or surroundings	17	0.7
Trips and Outings	13	0.6
Extra-curricular activities	79	3.4
Race relations	40	1.7
Teaching about other races/cultures	18	0.8
Teachers help us to get on	15	0.6
Negative comment e.g. when its closed	163	7.0
Break and/or dinnertime	196	8.4
School meals	55	2.4

25. Please write here what you dislike most about school.
  (x1.1 for percentage of 2,029 pupils responding)

		Percentage
No comment	297	12.8
Nothing	76	3.3
Other pupils; bullies, etc.	347	14.9
Teachers in general	155	6.7
Some (e.g. specific) teachers	513	22.1
Lessons in general	95	4.1
Some (e.g. specific) lessons	509	21.9
General ethos	45	1.9
General relationships	49	2.1
Quality or range of lessons	20	0.9
Quality or range of facilities	26	1.1
Buildings or surroundings	129	5.5
Absence of trips or outings	10	0.4
Lack of extra-curricular activities	4	0.2

Race relations	95	4.1
Teachers don't help good relationships	8	0.3
Boring	43	1.8
Uniform	77	3.3
'Everything'	48	2.1
Discipline, punishments, etc.	53	2.3
Too many holidays	2	0.1
Too many Muslims/Bengalis, etc.	17	0.7
Minority pupils dominate	16	0.7
Having to do school work	72	3.1
General pupil behaviour	114	4.9
School rules	224	9.6
Homework	143	6.1
Assemblies	21	0.9
School dinners	67	2.9
Breaks/dinnertime	56	2.4
Exams	7	0.3
Minorities treated better	2	0.1
Sitting beside boys	1	0.0
Loneliness	2	0.1

26. If there is anything else you would like to say about your school or the different groups in it, please write it here.

(x4.7 for percentage of 496 pupils responding)

		Percentage
No comment	1,830	78.7
General positive comment	77	3.3
General negative comment	75	3.2
Positive comment about race relations	76	3.3
Negative comment about race relations	83	3.6
Positive comment about teachers	16	0.7
Negative comment about teachers	63	2.7
Positive comment about lessons	11	0.5
Negative comment about lessons	17	0.7
Positive comment about other pupils	35	1.5
Negative comment about other pupils	59	2.5
Being picked on, bullied, etc.	25	1.1
Dislike of particular pupils	31	1.3
Minorities not treated fairly	3	0.1
Minorities treated better than others	12	0.5
Too many minority pupils	5	0.2
Negative statement about trips, etc.	7	0.3
School uniform	3	0.1
Absence of minority foods	2	0.1

PART B

Q.6 Perception of the student's knowledge of other pupils

Answer	Caribbean	Others	Bangladeshi *	Others	Muslims *	Others	Ethnic Minorities *	Others
Lot	5.2	6.4	16.5	5.1	15.7	3.9	8.9	3.6
Some	19.0	17.2	29.9	15.7	29.1	14.1	21.1	13.3
Most	30.7	33.0	23.6	34.0	30.3	33.6	32.7	33.1
Not much	35.3	34.0	19.3	35.9	17.3	38.6	28.8	39.9
Nothing	6.5	7.8	8.3	7.6	6.5	8.0	6.7	8.8

Q.7 Perception of other students' knowledge of them

Answer	Caribbean *	Others	Bangladeshi	Others	Muslims *	Others	Ethnic Minorities *	Others
Lot	7.2	12.3	13.4	11.8	10.2	12.5	9.9	14.2
Quite a bit	38.6	48.2	46.1	47.8	48.0	47.5	46.3	48.9
Not much	35.9	29.0	32.3	29.1	34.1	28.2	32.1	26.6
Nothing	12.4	8.2	5.5	8.9	5.9	9.2	9.2	7.8

* Indicates statistical significance at or above the 99 per cent level

Q.8 Perception of help given by teachers to increase understanding

Answer	Caribbean *	Others	Bangladeshi *	Others	Muslims *	Others	Ethnic Minorities *	Others
Lot	16.3	20.1	42.1	17.1	35.8	15.5	24.2	15.2
Quite a bit	31.4	43.2	37.8	43.0	37.6	43.8	39.8	45.3
Not much	34.0	25.8	13.8	27.9	17.7	28.7	24.4	28.5
Nothing	15.7	9.3	4.7	10.3	7.5	10.3	9.6	9.8

Q.9 Perception of inter-ethnic relationships

Answer	Caribbean	Others	Bangladeshi *	Others	Muslims	Others	Ethnic Minorities *	Others
Well	31.4	28.3	20.1	29.6	26.8	29.0	25.2	31.9
Quite well	61.4	58.7	64.2	58.3	60.8	58.4	60.0	57.8
Not well	5.2	9.0	10.6	8.5	8.9	8.7	10.7	6.7
Not at all	2.0	2.3	2.0	2.4	1.4	2.6	2.3	2.4

Q.10 Frequency of being called names

Answer	Caribbean	Others	Bangladeshi *	Others	Muslims *	Others	Ethnic Minorities	Others
Never	28.1	21.2	16.5	22.2	15.9	23.2	19.7	23.7
Not often	58.2	59.5	57.5	59.6	61.8	58.7	60.1	58.6
Quite a lot	7.8	13.9	18.5	12.9	15.0	13.1	14.1	12.9
All the time	3.9	4.0	4.7	4.0	4.9	3.8	4.3	3.8

* Indicates statistical significance at or above the 99 per cent level

Q.11 The reasons for being called names

Answer	Caribbean * Others		Bangladeshi * Others		Muslims * Others		Ethnic Minorities * Others	
Girl	7.2	8.8	7.5	8.8	5.9	9.4	7.8	9.6
Boy	3.3	4.1	3.9	4.1	4.3	4.0	4.2	3.9
Religion	2.0	8.7	23.6	6.3	25.4	3.6	13.3	2.8
Race/colour	23.5	18.5	48.8	15.1	45.1	11.7	28.6	8.3
Language	2.0	7.3	26.0	4.6	24.4	2.3	12.1	1.5
Additional:								
Background	3.3	1.8	2.4	1.9	2.4	1.8	2.2	1.7
Features	11.8	12.1	3.1	13.2	4.3	14.2	8.7	15.8
Dress/appearance	5.9	3.6	0.0	4.2	0.8	4.5	3.3	4.3
Name	1.3	2.5	3.1	2.4	2.8	2.3	2.8	2.1
In fun	3.3	2.9	1.6	3.1	2.0	3.2	2.5	3.4
No reason	2.0	4.9	1.6	5.1	1.6	5.5	3.3	6.1
Not true	0.0	0.7	0.0	0.8	0.0	0.9	0.2	1.2
Work	0.0	0.8	0.0	10.8	0.2	0.9	0.2	1.2

Q.12 Feelings about name-calling

Answer	Caribbean * Others		Bangladeshi * Others		Muslims * Others		Ethnic Minorities * Others	
Not bothered	45.1	45.8	24.9	48.3	31.6	49.5	40.4	51.4
Sad	3.3	9.3	20.5	7.5	16.5	6.9	10.1	7.6
Angry	17.6	17.5	35.4	15.3	29.1	14.4	21.9	12.9
Left out	5.2	7.4	6.7	7.3	9.1	6.8	7.7	6.8
Get own back	26.1	21.2	15.7	22.2	21.1	21.6	24.1	18.7

* Indicates statistical significance at or above the 99 per cent level

Q.13 Frequency of student calling others names

Answer	Caribbean	Others	Bangladeshi * Others		Muslims * Others		Ethnic Minorities * Others	
Never	24.2	26.0	34.6	24.8	33.0	23.9	27.0	24.6
Not often	64.7	62.2	50.0	63.9	55.8	64.2	61.3	63.6
Quite a lot	5.2	7.1	7.1	7.0	5.9	7.3	6.4	7.6
All the time	2.0	2.8	4.3	2.6	2.2	2.9	3.0	2.5

Q.14 Reasons for calling others names

Answer	Caribbean	Others	Bangladeshi	Others	Muslims	Others	Ethnic Minorities	Others
Girl	6.5	4.1	7.1	3.9	5.3	4.0	5.0	3.5
Boy	6.5	5.4	6.3	5.4	6.9	5.1	5.9	5.1
Religion	5.9	5.2	6.3	5.2	6.5	5.0	5.7	4.9
Race/colour	7.8	7.8	10.6	7.5	9.6	7.4	9.1	6.5
Language	5.9	5.5	6.3	5.4	5.5	5.5	6.1	4.9
Additional:								
Background	0.7	1.8	1.2	1.8	1.0	1.9	2.2	1.2
Features	6.5	4.1	2.8	4.5	2.2	4.9	4.3	4.3
Dress/appearance	3.3	1.2	0.0	1.5	0.6	1.6	1.3	1.3
Name	0.0	1.3	1.6	1.2	2.4	0.9	1.8	0.6
In fun	9.2	5.1	1.6	5.8	2.4	6.1	4.3	6.5
No reason	7.8	7.9	4.7	8.3	4.5	8.8	6.1	9.8
Getting own back	11.8	16.6	15.4	16.4	16.9	16.1	16.3	16.1

* Indicates statistical significance at or above the 99 per cent level

Q.15 Student's perception of the feelings of those being called names

Answer	Caribbean	Others	Bangladeshi *	Others	Muslims *	Others	Ethnic Minorities *	Others
Not bothered	33.3	31.2	19.7	32.7	23.6	33.4	28.5	34.3
Sad	11.8	14.6	20.1	13.8	15.4	14.2	15.7	13.1
Angry	17.0	15.9	21.7	15.3	18.5	15.3	17.0	14.8
Left out	6.5	8.6	8.3	8.5	7.5	8.7	9.0	7.9
Get own back	28.1	22.4	12.2	24.0	16.7	24.4	22.4	23.2

Q.16 Frequency of jokes told about the student's race, religion or colour.

Answer	Caribbean	Others	Bangladeshi *	Others	Muslims	Others	Ethnic Minorities	Others
Never	41.8	34.1	20.1	36.4	22.6	37.9	30.6	39.0
Not often	37.9	45.9	49.6	44.9	48.6	44.5	47.3	43.3
A lot	10.5	13.9	19.3	13.0	20.5	11.8	14.9	12.3
All the time	5.9	2.9	5.9	2.8	4.1	2.8	3.8	2.4

* Indicates statistical significance at or above the 99 per cent level

Q.17 Feelings of the student

Answer	Caribbean	Others	Bangladeshi *	Others	Muslims *	Others	Ethnic Minorities *	Others
Ignore	24.8	33.1	35.8	32.1	36.8	31.4	33.1	31.9
Find funny	27.5	25.3	16.1	26.6	18.5	27.3	24.2	26.8
Sad	2.6	4.5	13.0	3.3	9.1	3.1	6.0	2.7
Angry	14.4	8.7	19.3	7.9	17.1	7.0	12.4	5.6
Left out	1.3	2.4	6.3	1.8	6.3	1.3	3.5	1.1
Get own back	9.8	9.4	14.6	8.8	15.0	7.9	12.0	6.7

Q.18 Frequency of telling jokes about other students' race/religion/colour

Answer	Caribbean	Others	Bangladeshi *	Others	Muslims	Others	Ethnic Minorities	Others
Never	53.6	50.9	51.6	51.0	52.6	50.7	51.7	50.4
Not often	37.9	39.9	34.3	40.5	36.8	40.6	38.7	41.0
A lot	2.0	5.4	6.3	5.1	4.7	5.3	5.1	5.3
All the time	3.3	1.2	2.0	1.3	1.2	1.4	1.6	1.1

* Indicates statistical significance at or above the 99 per cent level

Q.19 How other students feel

Answer	Caribbean	Others	Bangladeshi	Others	Muslims	Others	Ethnic Minorities	Others
Ignore	13.1	15.6	13.0	15.8	15.0	15.6	16.0	14.9
Find funny	24.8	21.6	15.4	22.6	18.5	22.7	20.8	23.0
Sad	5.9	8.1	7.9	8.0	6.7	8.3	8.1	7.9
Angry	3.3	8.7	13.4	7.7	10.8	7.7	8.4	8.3
Left out	2.6	3.9	2.8	3.9	3.5	3.9	3.9	3.6
Get own back	10.5	10.0	11.8	9.8	11.4	9.7	10.9	9.1

Q.20 Frequency of being bullied

Answer	Caribbean	Others	Bangladeshi *	Others	Muslims *	Others	Ethnic Minorities	Others
Never	69.3	56.4	48.0	58.4	50.4	59.1	56.0	58.6
Not often	21.6	35.2	38.2	33.8	38.6	33.1	34.5	34.0
A lot	3.9	3.9	5.9	3.6	4.9	3.6	4.2	3.5
All the time	1.3	1.8	2.0	1.5	1.8	1.7	1.9	1.6

* Indicates statistical significance at or above the 99 per cent level

Index